223.44

YOUR PRIVACY

Protecting It
in a Nosy World

YOUR PRIVACY

Protecting It in a Nosy World

Edward F. Dolan

COBBLEHILL BOOKS
DUTTON   NEW YORK

Library of Congress Cataloging-in-Publication Data
Dolan, Edward F., date
Your privacy : protecting it in a nosy world / Edward F. Dolan.
p.   cm.
Includes bibliographical references and index.
ISBN 0-525-65187-X
1. Privacy, Right of—United States.   I. Title.
JC596.2.U5D65   1995   323.44'8'0973—dc20   94-14168   CIP

Published in the United States by Cobblehill Books,
an affiliate of Dutton Children's Books,
a division of Penguin Books USA Inc.,
375 Hudson Street, New York, New York 10014

Designed by Joseph Rutt
Printed in the United States of America
First Edition   10 9 8 7 6 5 4 3 2 1

ACKNOWLEDGMENTS

For their kindness and cooperation in providing me with research materials needed for the preparation of this book or patiently answering my questions, I am deeply indebted to the national headquarters of the American Civil Liberties Union; Maurice Lafferty, retired associate professor of criminal justice, College of Marin, Marin County, California; attorney Robert Bennett McCreadie of Marin County; and Robert Ellis Smith, the publisher of the newsletter *Privacy Journal* and the author of *Privacy: How to Protect What's Left of It*.

I also wish to acknowledge permission to quote from the following sources:

Privacy: How to Protect What's Left of It, by Robert Ellis Smith, Doubleday, a division of Bantam, Doubleday, Dell Publishing Group, Inc., 1980.

ACLU Briefing Paper: Drug Testing in the Workplace, American Civil Liberties Union.

ACLU Briefing Paper: The Rights of Employees, American Civil Liberties Union.

CONTENTS

CHAPTER ONE

THIS NOSY WORLD

Winston Smith lives in a totalitarian state called Oceania. His mind and the minds of all his fellow citizens are strictly controlled by the government's Thought Police. When he is found to harbor thoughts against the government and its leader, Big Brother, he is arrested, tortured, and left broken in body and spirit.

There is no such person as Winston Smith, no such state as Oceania, and no such dictator as Big Brother. All three are the inventions of British writer George Orwell and are found in his novel, *1984*. The book was published in 1949 and has been famous ever since for its warnings of the dangers promised by totalitarian societies.

Orwell speaks of a variety of these dangers in *1984*, among them the use of hate propaganda and brainwashing. One of the most tragic and commonplace of the lot is the lack of privacy. Winston Smith knows that the Thought Police, using wiretap and television devices, can "plug in" on him—

and any other citizen—at any time of the day or night to listen to his every word and watch (except in the dark) his every move. Wherever he goes in the course of his day, he sees large television sets. They deliver government propaganda messages and, time and again, show the face of Big Brother. The dictator's image is always accompanied by the warning that he is watching the people and knows all that is happening in their lives.

Happily, we Americans do not live in an Oceania-like society that denies us our privacy. We have always looked on the right to privacy as one of our most treasured possessions. Ever since our country's first days, we have had the tradition of not "poking our noses" into the private lives of others and insisting that others—from our next-door neighbors to the federal government—not "poke their noses" into our private lives. Historians credit the tradition with making all our freedoms work. It has enabled us to think, speak, worship, and act in our own way and ignore the many people and groups that would like to make us think, speak, worship, and act as they do. It has always demanded that our individuality be respected and that we respect the individuality of others.

Violations of our right to privacy are known as invasions of privacy. It is obvious that, if this invaluable right is to be preserved, we must constantly safeguard it against all such intrusions. But, while we don't live in Winston Smith's Oceania, Americans everywhere are realizing that we do live in a time when it is becoming increasingly difficult to protect ourselves. They feel that our privacy is being invaded today in myriad ways, all of them having to do with the way modern life is lived.

OUR INVADED PRIVACY: BITS OF PERSONAL INFORMATION

Let's begin with what happens to our privacy when we deal with business firms, public and private agencies, and the government. We are called on to give up bits of personal information about ourselves at every turn of the way. In our business dealings, this happens when we do such things as apply for a job, open a bank account, buy something on credit, or obtain a credit card. It happens when we apply for a driver's license, seek a student loan, ask for welfare assistance, or enroll in a school.

The information that we provide ranges from our name, address, and age to details about our earnings, our health, our personal outlooks, and our past activities. Some people look on the demand for the most innocent of this information as an invasion of their privacy; some, for example, believe that their age is nobody's business but their own; others don't want their telephone numbers known to anyone but their closest friends. Most of us, however, do not mind surrendering certain basic information because we understand that it is needed for the smooth running of a business or other type of organization.

We realize, for example, that car dealers need to protect themselves by checking into our income and our history of meeting our bills before allowing us to purchase their newest van on credit. It's the only way they have of gauging whether we have the ability to pay off a very sizable debt or can be trusted not to run out on our obligation.

But there is hardly a one of us who is not angered—no, outraged—when we hear of what happens to so much of the information. We feel that our privacy is being violated when the information we provide on, say, a job or credit card application is then put to some extra use without our knowledge or consent.

This "extra use" is one of the most widespread of today's privacy problems. Here's one major example of how it works. Suppose that, when filling out an application for a job with the International Widget Corporation, you're questioned about your hobbies. You give swimming, camping, and bowling as your answer and then soon find yourself besieged with "junk mail" ads and telephone calls from companies selling gear for swimmers, campers, and bowlers. What has happened is that International Widget has put your name on a list of job applicants interested in these sports and has sold or rented it to a string of companies specializing in the manufacture and sale of gear for them. You can't help but feel that International Widget has violated your privacy by arranging for you to be swamped in a flood of unwanted sales pitches.

International Widget is far from being alone in insulting our privacy in this way and reaping a profit from it. Stores, manufacturers, banks, charitable groups, telephone companies, and government bodies—all compile lists and sell or rent them to companies and organizations that can put them to profitable use. The lists are varied in their content, but all share a common aim—to pinpoint the people most likely to buy a certain product or service. Some lists, as was International Widget's, contain the names of people with specific interests. Some contain the names of people living in particular areas, or those in certain age groups, or the names of those with substantial incomes.

The business of using the lists to get in touch with you

and sell you something is known variously as telemarketing (when the telephone is used), direct marketing, or direct mail marketing. Some companies, in addition to using material provided by International Widget and others, develop lists of their own from information collected from their customers and even from telephone books; buy a set of tires from an automotive store and you can be pretty sure that you'll soon receive an advertisement about a sale the store is holding. In recent years, the telemarketing and direct marketing industry has become a major and highly profitable one in the United States. It is estimated to earn at least $2 billion annually.

Many lists are compiled for other than direct and telemarketing purposes. Some are meant to help manufacturers develop products of broad sales appeal. Some are assembled by local and national credit institutions—known as credit bureaus—and are made available to any concern that sells its merchandise on credit and wants to know whether its customers are likely to pay off or default on their debts; when your name appears on such lists, it is accompanied by your history of meeting earlier debts. Still others provide charitable organizations with the names of people thought to be good prospects for contributions—chiefly because they are known to have a history of charitable donations. It is common practice for some charitable groups to sell or rent their lists to fellow groups.

The gathering of information for commercial and other purposes is rapidly turning the United States into a records-keeping nation. Records of all sorts are stored everywhere. Schools keep records of our attendance, attitudes, and behavior. Employers maintain records of our performance at work. Prospective employers gather records from various sources to help them judge whether they wish to hire us. Insurance companies continually update their records of everything from our health problems to traffic citations and automobile accidents—all for the purpose of keeping track of their profits and losses and gauging whether we need to be charged higher rates in the future. Local and national credit bureaus likewise constantly update their records. The U.S. government, for reasons we'll discuss in a later chapter, has amassed the greatest number of records of all.

Time magazine recently reported that in 1982 (the latest year in which a count was made), the federal government held some 3.5 billion files on individual Americans—an average of fifteen files per person. The number of government files is certain to have increased during the years since 1982.

Most of us don't like the idea of having so many organizations know so much about us. We feel that we are being—or have already been—stripped bare. And, though some of the records are supposed to be confidential, there is the fear that all the information can be passed from organization to organization and turn our lives into an "open book" for too many people.

OUR INVADED PRIVACY: MODERN TECHNOLOGY

Making matters even worse is the fact that there is technological equipment on the scene today that was unheard of in earlier years. Much of it makes the gathering and storing of information about us all too easy. Of all such gear, the computer looms as the greatest threat to our privacy.

There was a time when the information we provided on applying for, say, a job or a driver's license was typed on a piece of paper and tucked away in a file cabinet. It could remain there for years and never reach the outside world. But not now. Today, any data that is collected about us in one place or another—and for any number of reasons—can be stored in computer banks across the nation. It can then easily come into the hands of businesses and government agencies so that it can be put to various uses. It can, of course, be sold or rented to them. It can be passed from one organization to another as a gesture of "friendly co-operation." Or, if it is of a highly confidential nature and not meant for public distribution, it can be stolen by a computer "hacker" who manages to break into the bank.

The computer is called the "super electronic device of the century." But it is joined by other gadgets that can—and have been made to—violate our privacy: devices that can be attached to our telephones to record our calls, wiretap "bugs" that can be concealed in our homes and pick up our private conversations, still and motion picture cameras that can photograph us from great distances or in the dark, and an especially popular device that has come on the market within recent years—the portable videotape camera with its ability not only to take our pictures but record our voices at the same time.

The videotape camera—or, as it is variously called, the video camera or camcorder—enables anyone to spy on us with greater ease than was earlier possible with still and hand-held motion picture cameras. It has shown itself to be a mixed blessing. On the one hand, amateur cameramen have taped dramatic and worthwhile news stories, such as heroic rescues during floods. It has also caught people in criminal acts, as was done when the doctors in a southwestern hospital began to suspect that a seven-month-old patient had been the victim of abuse by her mother. They concealed a video camera in the infant's room and video-taped the mother as she attempted to smother her daughter. But, on the other hand, the camera has been used for purposes that either seem to be or are clearly violations of privacy.

One of the clearest and cruelest violations came to light some years ago in Texas, where a young woman was secretly videotaped as she made love to her boyfriend. The taping was done by a camera that had been hidden in the room by some of her boyfriend's pals. When the young woman learned of the tape and that it was being shown in her boyfriend's fraternity house, she sued him and his friends for invasion of privacy and won a court judgment of $1 million.

In this day and age of secret videotaping, it is possible that you have been taped without your knowledge when out shopping. Ever since the late 1980s, customers have been taped while they decided on the purchases that they would make in stores, shopping malls, and automobile agencies. The videotaping is done by research firms and is intended to help merchants and manufacturers better understand what prompts a consumer to make a purchase and to buy certain products. The information is garnered from such details as the way a consumer dresses, the questions he or she asks, and the way he or she reacts to certain colors and styles of packaging. The information helps the manufacturers to turn out popular products, and the merchants to display them in more appealing ways. Both have argued that no one's privacy has been violated because the tapings have been done in public places and have involved an innocent activity that could not be of embarrassment to the consumer. But countless Americans have disagreed and have been angered on learning that they have been turned into "television performers" without their knowledge while going about their day's shopping.

OUR INVADED PRIVACY: A SOCIAL PROBLEM

Along with having our privacy threatened by today's technological equipment and widespread information gathering, we live with an odd social problem. Ours is a time in which our traditional love of privacy is being abandoned on many fronts. That respect is being equaled by a love for gossip and the profits that gossip can reap. Daily, we're fed a diet of newspaper, magazine, radio, and television accounts of the private lives of celebrities, with the accent so often put on the ugly aspects of those lives. Publishers hand us one book after another in which celebrities "tell all" about themselves, their families, and their friends—again, with the "all" often being of an ugly nature. Several times a day, television talk shows feature celebrities and people we've never heard of who are willing to chat about the most private matters in their lives—their emotional upheavals, their sexual practices, their problems with their families—all of them subjects that, in the past, would never have been fit for mention in public or even within many families.

This odd social problem has reached out to touch our own privacy. There is probably not a one of us who isn't familiar with one of today's most popular phrases: "Let it all hang out." In myriad ways, we're all pressured to do exactly *that* daily, to tell all about our own lives and private feelings. We're pressured indirectly by the news reports, the talk eshows, and the "tell-all" books that have made the revealing of personal secrets such a national fad and have left so many of us with the feeling that we're out of step with the modern world if we don't do the same thing. And we're pressured directly by many of our friends and others (perhaps a school counselor, perhaps a club or gang leader, perhaps a religious figure) who want us to tell them all about ourselves for our "own good."

Despite all of today's invasions of our privacy, we are not yet Winston Smiths and we don't yet live in a suffocating society such as Oceania. But there is no doubt that we do live in a nosy world and that countless Americans see the ever-growing number of invasions as one of today's most pervasive and dangerous problems—one that can, at the least, make us angry and uncomfortable, and, at the worst, change the way life is lived in our country.

In this book, we're going to talk about what you can do now as a young person, and later as an adult, to protect yourself and to speak out when the world sticks its nose too far into your privacy at home, at school, at work, and wherever you go in life. In guarding your own privacy and speaking out on its behalf, you'll also be guarding the privacy of everyone around you.

But, first, we need to see exactly what is meant by the right to privacy and how it is already safeguarded in the United States. It is protected by our Constitution, our laws, and the decisions reached by our courts. Only when we know the protections that are available to us can we be in the best position to defend ourselves and all those around us against any attack on one of our most valuable and cherished possessions.

CHAPTER TWO
PRIVACY AND THE CONSTITUTION

Many years ago, a noted American jurist, U.S. Supreme Court Justice Louis D. Brandeis (1856–1941), defined the right to privacy in the simplest of terms. He called it "the right of the individual to be let alone."

But is there actually such a right in our country? The question must be asked because, unlike the freedoms of speech, religion, and the press, our right to privacy is not specifically mentioned in the United States Constitution. This omission caused some legal experts in years past to say that, though the right is a highly desirable one and should be granted to all the people, it is nevertheless not actually a constitutionally guaranteed one.

Others, among them another highly respected U.S. Supreme Court justice, William O. Douglas (1898–1980), disagreed and argued that the right is indeed guaranteed. He pointed out that it is present by implication in five of the first ten amendments to the Constitution, as set forth in the

Bill of Rights. The five are the First, Third, Fourth, Fifth, and Ninth Amendments.

Justice Douglas went on to say that the right "is older than the Bill of Rights" and that it exists in the shadow of all our other constitutional guarantees.

PRESENT BY IMPLICATION

Today, Justice Douglas's view prevails and the right to privacy is recognized as constitutionally guaranteed because of its presence by implication in the five Amendments. But how, exactly, do they imply its presence? No more than a brief look at each is needed to find the answer:

The First Amendment grants us not only the freedom of press, but forbids Congress to make any law "abridging the freedom of speech . . . or the right of the people peaceably to assemble . . ."

Robert Ellis Smith, the publisher of the widely respected newsletter, *Privacy Times*, one of the nation's leading authorities in privacy matters, explains in a single sentence how the right is present here. In his book, *Privacy: How to Protect What's Left of It*, he writes; "You can't very well exercise freedom in political expression and association unless you have a right to think what you wish and meet with whomever you wish, free of governmental intrusion."

The First Amendment, however, brings us immediately to a basic point that must always be remembered concerning the right of privacy. Like many other of our rights, it is not an absolute one. It has limits—limits that are imposed on it by the rights of others. For one, we are entitled to give a private party and invite to it anyone we wish, but our right to privacy vanishes and the people's rights to a safe community and the protection of their belongings takes over when the partygoers tumble drunkenly out into the street and begin damaging and destroying the neighboring properties. For another, we lose much of our right to privacy when we engage in a public activity. The First Amendment gives us the right to assemble peaceably, but we cannot complain that our privacy is being violated when a news photographer takes our picture while we are participating in a peaceful street demonstration. People have the right to know what the demonstration is about and what is happening. The press has the right and the duty to tell them.

The Third Amendment holds that "No soldier shall, in time of peace, be quartered in any house, without the consent of the owner."

Though it refers only to the housing of soldiers, the Amendment leaves no doubt that the authors of the Bill of Rights wanted to make certain that a family's most private possession—its home—would be left free of all intrusions by the authorities.

But, again, we need to remember that our right here is not an absolute one. The prohibition against housing soldiers in one's home applies only in peacetime. If necessary for the nation's defense, the local or federal government can take over private homes for military use in times of war.

The Fourth Amendment specifies that it is "the right of the people to be secure in their persons, houses, papers, and effects against unreasonable searches and seizures."

This Amendment takes a major step beyond the safeguard provided by the Third. In guaranteeing the safety of our homes and our persons from unwarranted intrusions, it protects us not only from military authorities but from all authorities who would take advantage of us. Of the five Amendments, the Fourth is said to give the strongest indication that the Constitution does indeed guarantee us the right to privacy.

The Amendment, however, protects us only against *unreasonable* searches and seizures. The authorities are permitted to conduct reasonable searches and seizures. But they must meet certain conditions before their actions can be considered reasonable and thus legal. We'll be talking of those conditions in Chapter Four.

The Fifth Amendment states that no person "shall be compelled in any criminal case to be a witness against himself."

Here is one area where our right to privacy is absolute. We cannot be punished for refusing to speak out against ourselves. The fact that we are entitled to remain silent and not be forced to damage ourselves when suspected of or charged with a criminal activity can leave no doubt that the authors of the Bill of Rights felt that there are aspects of our lives that may not be intruded upon by the authorities, no matter now vital our testimony against ourselves may be to the government or the public interest.

Our freedom to refuse to testify against ourselves applies

not only to court cases but also to investigative hearings conducted by governmental bodies, such as the hearings that the U.S. Congress has conducted at times into suspected criminal and subversive activities in the country.

The Ninth Amendment has often been called the "catch-all" or "safety-net" amendment. It states simply that "The enumeration in the Constitution, of certain rights, shall not be construed to deny or disparage others retained by the people."

What is meant here, of course, is that the authorities are prohibited from claiming that we do not hold certain obvious rights, such as the right to privacy, simply because they are not specifically mentioned in the Constitution.

There is another amendment that must be mentioned—**the Fourteenth.** It was enacted in the wake of the Civil War and stipulates that:

"No State shall make or enforce any law which shall abridge the privileges or immunities of citizens of the United States; nor shall any State deprive any person of life, liberty, or property, without due process of law; nor deny to any person within its jurisdiction the equal protection of the laws."

The initial purpose of the Fourteenth Amendment was to prevent any state from passing laws that would deprive the newly freed slaves of their rights as citizens. Since then, it has been employed as a safeguard against the enactment of any state law that will abridge the rights of any citizen, regardless of his or her color.

In 1973, the Fourteenth Amendment played a role in two of the most controversial privacy cases ever to come before the U.S. Supreme Court—*Roe v. Wade* and *Doe v. Bolton.* Each dealt with a woman's right to have an abortion, a right that had previously been denied to her. The decisions rendered by the Court in the two cases legalized abortion in the United States and triggered a controversy that continues to this day. Both cases will be described in the next chapter.

A CHANGING NATION

When the Bill of Rights was written, its authors were not thinking of how an individual's privacy could be invaded by his or her fellow citizens and business concerns. Rather, they were out to protect everyone against the chance of having the newly formed U.S. government fall into the wrong hands and begin to intrude too much on the lives of the people. Still vivid in their memories was the stern and intrusive rule that the British had imposed on the colonies in the years leading up to the Revolutionary War. They remembered how the colonists had been forced to quarter red-coated troops in their homes. They remembered how the people had been made to stand by as the British searched their homes for evidence of illegal activities or for clues that members of the family were plotting rebellion against the Crown.

Actually, at the time the Bill of Rights took shape, there was no reason to be worried about invasions of one's privacy by fellow citizens and business operations. Several facts of life in the young United States accounted for this happy situation.

For one, the country was chiefly rural in nature; people were not crowded together in giant cities as so many are today and so were not likely to intrude on one another's private lives. Next, there was not yet on the scene all the modern equipment—from the camera to the computer— that is now making it so easy to violate anyone's privacy. Finally, there was that national tradition of "not poking your nose into the private lives of others" and insisting that they not "poke their noses" into yours. The tradition could clearly be seen in the newspapers and the books of the eighteenth and nineteenth centuries. They did not devote themselves to gossip and to "tell-all" confessions by public figures.

By the 1890s, however, the nation was experiencing a mighty change so far as privacy was concerned. Responsible for the change was the emergence of such technological marvels as the telephone, the high-speed camera, and the linotype machine. Many people viewed them as threats to their hitherto untroubled privacy. The telephone could ring at any time and interrupt them at whatever they were doing. Unlike the cameras of the past, which required long minutes to imprint an image on glass or paper, the new camera could do the job in an instant and was thus able to photograph people as they worked and played—and could do so from a distance. The linotype machine enabled newspapers to set print at a speed unheard of when the words had to be set by hand, one letter at a time. Consequently, the papers were now producing larger and larger editions. Many editors, to fill an increasing number of pages, were turning more and more to gossip items.

Two New England attorneys were deeply troubled by the

situation, especially the burgeoning number of gossipy newspaper items. They felt that the time had come to attend to a problem that had never before been a problem for the American people. The time had come to do something about protecting everyone's privacy.

CHAPTER THREE

PRIVACY AND THE LAW

The two attorneys were Samuel D. Warren and Louis D. Brandeis. Warren was a professor of law at Harvard University. Brandeis, who defined the right to privacy as the right "to be let alone," would later serve on the U.S. Supreme Court, from 1916 to 1939. Their concern was triggered by Warren's wife.

Mrs. Warren was a socially prominent woman who enjoyed giving large parties in her home. But, unlike many socialite hostesses, she cherished her privacy and angrily charged that it had been violated when a Boston newspaper reported on the details of her parties, naming her guests and describing the food she served them. She was especially irked by the fact that the details had been published without her consent.

Both her husband and Brandeis agreed that her privacy had indeed been violated. Worried that people would be subjected to a growing number of such violations in the coming years, the two attorneys wrote an article for the *Harvard Law Review* in which they condemned the press for its love of gossip. They remarked acidly that "gossip is no longer the resource of the idle and the vicious, but has become a trade, which is pursued with industry as well as effrontery" and that "instantaneous photography and newspaper enterprise have invaded the sacred precincts of private and domestic life." From there, the two went on to predict that future technological wonders, plus the nation's increasing population, would surely pose a threat one day to everyone's privacy. They urged the nation to develop a set of laws and legal outlooks that would safeguard the privacy of all Americans.

Their article triggered widespread discussion in the U.S. legal community and helped to lead to two important developments in our century. First, there was the recognition that the right to privacy is a constitutionally guaranteed one due to its presence by implication in the Bill of Rights. Second, the nation's courts and legislators settled on the ways—four in all—in which one's privacy can be invaded.

FOUR INVASIONS

These four invasions are not criminal offenses. Rather, they are civil offenses—or torts, as they are technically known—meaning that you are entitled to go to court and seek redress for the intrusions. Usually, you can seek redress in two ways, either one or the other or both. You may sue to receive money for the damages done by the party responsible for the invasion, or you may ask the court to order the invading party to stop or stay away from you.

Now, just what are the four? Here they are, followed by a brief explanation of what each entails. Your privacy is judged to be invaded when someone or an organization:

- Intrudes on your solitude.
- Discloses private facts about you that you find embarrassing.
- Releases publicity about you that causes the public to see you in a "false light."
- Uses your name or picture for personal profit without your consent.

An Intrusion on Your Solitude

Let's say that you are a television star. A news photographer follows you wherever you go and snaps so many pictures of what you're doing that you finally lose patience and take him to court.

As a celebrity, you surrender much of your right to privacy. Due to your fame, your life is a matter of public interest. You are newsworthy. People want to know—and, especially if you are involved in political activities, feel they need to know—as much about you as possible. The press, under its constitutional freedom, holds the right to report to them on your public and private activities. That right includes the right to take your photograph.

But you maintain that the photographer is pursuing you too relentlessly. You may go to court and ask that he be made to stop or keep his distance. Your argument is that, even though famous and newsworthy, you are still entitled to a reasonable expectation of privacy and freedom from harassment, and that both are being violated.

Your lawsuit here is identical to the one that Jacqueline Kennedy Onassis, the widow of President John F. Kennedy, brought against a news photographer in 1973. The judge, agreeing with the above argument, ruled in favor of Mrs. Onassis. He ordered the photographer to remain at least twenty-five feet away from her and her children at all times, even when they were out in a public place.

The Disclosure of Embarrassing Personal Facts

You are campaigning to be elected the mayor of your town. A reporter from the local newspaper comes to your home to interview you. While there, he noses about the house and then writes an article in which he indicates that you're a slovenly person. He reports finding baskets of dirty clothes near your washing machine and describes your kitchen sink as overflowing with unwashed dishes. Off to court you go, charging that the news item caused you deep embarrassment.

When disclosing private facts, the press is said to be on safe ground when it reports them fairly and accurately and when their disclosure is of benefit or legitimate interest to the public. In some instances, this applies to embarrassing facts. For example, the revelation that a member of Congress once used illegal drugs in his home can help voters decide whether he is fit to represent them or should be voted out of office.

But you argue that your case is different. In reporting on your careless housekeeping, the reporter did not reveal anything of benefit or legitimate interest to the public and did nothing but embarrass you. You have every right to sue, even though the facts may be painfully true. And you may do so, regardless of whether you're a famous or completely unknown person.

When considering your suit, however, the court will require that it meet two standards. First, you must show that the facts are indeed private; your case will suffer if the court, for instance, hears that they are already known to the whole town. Second, you must show that the facts have actually been made public. This means that they must have reached a greater segment of the public than, say, just two or three people.

Publicity That Puts You in a "False Light"

You're attending a party, perhaps in a public hall, perhaps in a friend's home. At one point in the evening, someone snaps your photograph as you are smoking a cigarette. The picture then finds its way into the local newspaper, where it is used in a report that marijuana was smoked at the party. The caption beneath the photograph states or insinuates that you are smoking a marijuana joint. You have grounds for a suit. The photo and caption have given the public a mistaken impression of you—have placed you in a "false light."

You may also sue for being placed in a "false light" if someone goes about impersonating you in public. The same holds true if someone forges your signature on a check or some other document.

The "false light" in which the marijuana photograph places you is embarrassing and damages your reputation.

But you are also permitted to sue when the information puts you in a very good "false light." It violates your privacy simply by being false and, as a result, causing you embarrassment or some other upset.

A case in point here involved the legendary baseball pitcher Warren Spahn, who joined the then Boston Braves in 1942, played in the major leagues for an amazing twenty-four years, and was voted into the Baseball Hall of Fame in 1973. In the 1960s, Spahn was made the subject of a biography which contained a string of falsehoods about his life and career. Some, such as an account of his service during World War II, were meant to make him look especially heroic. Others concerned his thoughts at points in his life—thoughts that the author certainly dreamed up on his own because not once during the writing of the book did he interview Spahn and others close to the pitcher.

The various falsehoods, which were written by an author who obviously got carried away by the idea of making his subject "look good," did not smear Spahn's personal or professional reputation. But, because they were false, they embarrassed and upset him deeply. He went to court and sued the author and the publisher.

Both defended themselves by saying that anything could be written about Spahn because the pitcher was a public figure. Further, they argued, Spahn had allowed the Braves to use his photograph for whatever publicity purposes they desired. In agreeing to such public use, he had implied that the author had the freedom to write as he did. The pitcher now had no right to say that his privacy had been invaded.

The judge rejected these arguments. He replied that Spahn, in allowing the Braves to use his photograph for publicity purposes, had not agreed that his life could be portrayed in a false way. The author and publisher had the right to turn out a genuine biography, but not the right to produce a "nonfactual novelization" of his life and career. In so doing, they had caused him "humiliation and mental anguish." The judge ordered that sales of the book be stopped and that Spahn be paid a sum of money to make up for the distress he had suffered.

The Use of Your Name or Picture for Personal Profit

While you are visiting a local amusement park, a video-tape camera focuses in on you and follows you from one ride to another. You're then astonished to see the tape on television as an advertisement for the park. No one had told you that you were being recorded. Nor had anyone asked for your permission before making you a television star for a few seconds. You have ample reason to sue for invasion of privacy. The park had used your picture for personal profit, something it is not allowed to do without your consent.

You would, of course, be helpless to sue had you given the park your permission, perhaps for some payment or perhaps simply because you are a satisfied customer or want to see yourself on television.

THE TYPES OF PRIVACY LAWS

In common with most of the laws that govern us, the laws that have been developed to protect our right to privacy are divided into three types—judge-made laws, statutory laws, and constitutionally based laws.

Judge-made Laws and Statutory Laws

There is a simple difference between these two types of laws. Statutory laws are put into writing and are known as statutes. They are enacted by local, state, and national legislators.

Judge-made laws, on the other hand, are not written down as statutes. Rather, they are laws that evolve from decisions made by judges in court cases. They usually come into being when a court is faced with a legal problem that is not covered by a statutory law but must be decided by the trial judge or by the state or federal supreme court. Very often, judge-made laws are later enacted into statutory laws.

A judge-made law sets a precedent—a guide—for any judges who are later faced with similar cases. Those judges may elect to use the precedent in their decisions if they think it wise and legal. They may ignore it if they find it weak or not applicable to the current case under their consideration. Here in America, a precedent set by a court in one state may be used in cases in other states.

The history of judge-made laws is centuries old. Those that are used in the United States first took shape in Great Britain when its people, from the kings to the lowliest of peasants, attempted to solve their various legal problems by placing them before a judge and letting him decide how they should be settled.

Though his decision in a case provided a solution to a legal question, it was not written down as a law. Rather, it served as a guide for settling future cases. In time, all the decisions came to be known collectively as English Common

Law—a body of basic rules and principles governing the legal rights of individuals, communities, and a nation.

English Common Law crossed the Atlantic to America with our first colonists. Today, Engish Common Law serves as the basis for the laws in all U.S. states except one.

(The one state that does not employ English Common Law is Louisiana. Its courts operate under the Napoleonic Code, which was developed in the early nineteenth century by Napoleon Bonaparte. The Code is a system of written laws, plus a series of rules governing courtroom procedures. In many ways, its laws are similar to those found in English Common Law.)

Judge-made law has played a role in the establishment of the four ways in which your privacy can be violated. For example, one of several early precedents involving the fourth violation was set in a 1905 case when a Georgia man sued an insurance company for invading his privacy by using his photograph without his permission in a newspaper advertisement. The insurance company argued that the ad had done no wrong because the right to privacy did not exist in Georgia—this because there were no laws pertaining to it in the state. There were no statutes on the books and there had never before been a privacy case tried in the state. The issue went to the Georgia Supreme Court, which decided in the man's favor. The court admitted that the right to privacy had never been determined in Georgia, but added that *this did not mean that it did not exist in the state*.

Statutory Laws

Statutory laws, you'll recall, are written laws that are known as statutes and that are enacted by local, state, and federal legislators. The laws that set the punishments for theft or govern the operation of a motor vehicle in your state provide commonplace examples of statutory laws.

The twentieth century has seen the passage of a number of statutory laws concerning privacy. For example, the following federal statutes rank high among the privacy measures that Congress has enacted within recent decades. We will be talking more of them in the coming chapters. For now, let us introduce them by naming them in the order in which they were passed into law:

- The Omnibus Crime Control and Safe Streets Act of 1968
- The Fair Credit Reporting Act of 1970
- The Right to Privacy Act of 1974
- The Family Educational Rights and Privacy Act of 1974
- The Video Privacy Protection Act of 1988

Practically all the states have statutes pertaining to privacy. Many are fashioned after the above U.S. laws for the sake of having federal and state laws match, with a number of the states adding protections beyond those stated in the federal statutes. Many other state privacy laws are similar to one another.

Virtually all the states carry statutes regarding trespass, which violates the privacy of a property owner or renter, because they consider trespassing illegal. To protect an adopted child's privacy, most states require that a new birth certificate be issued showing the child's adoptive name and that the original certificate then be sealed so that it cannot be seen by the public. (Birth certificates are public documents and can be made available to interested parties; the original birth certificate of an adopted child can be opened only by means of a court order.) Practically all the states maintain statutes protecting the privacy of the "doctor-patient" relationship, meaning that physicians may not be forced to give testimony in court about medical facts that were told to them in confidence. A physician, however, is free to provide these facts voluntarily.

Though many of the state laws are similar, just as many vary from state to state. In their specifics, the laws protecting the "doctor-patient" relationship differ greatly among the states; Pennsylvania, unlike some other states, protects the relationship only if the facts to be revealed in court are damaging to the patient. A number of states have privacy laws that are not found elsewhere. On the books in New York, for example, is a law that would never cross Florida's mind: it regulates the use of snowmobiles so that they will not disturb nearby residents.

Constitutionally Based Laws

Constitutionally based laws are types of judge-made laws. They come into being when state supreme courts decide on the constitutionality of the laws in their states—and when the United States Supreme Court decides on matters involving the constitutionality of either federal or state laws.

Over the years, the U.S. Supreme Court has issued decisions on a variety of privacy questions. Three have concerned what many people consider to be among the most private of matters—sexual practices within a marriage and a woman's right to choose to have an abortion.

The first of the trio came before the Court in 1965 and was called *Griswold v. Connecticut*. Brought by Mrs. Estelle Griswold and a Dr. Buxton, a professor of medicine, the case sought to overturn an 1879 Connecticut law that prohibited the use of birth control devices and called for the prosecution and punishment not only of those who used them but also of anyone who provided information concerning their use.

On the grounds that they were violating the decades-old law, Mrs. Griswold and Dr. Buxton had been arrested and fined $100 in 1961 for distributing contraceptive information to married couples at a birth control clinic they had founded in the city of New Haven. After their conviction had been upheld by two state courts, they took their case to the Supreme Court.

The Court overturned their convictions and ruled the Connecticut law to be unconstitutional. The Court's decision was written by Justice William O. Douglas, who remarked that the presence of the right to privacy by implication in the Bill of Rights established "zones of privacy" in every person's life. The Connecticut law, he commented, granted the state excessive powers to intrude on one's privacy and, as a result, invaded a sacrosanct privacy zone—the sexual relations between husband and wife.

Two of the most controversial privacy cases ever to come before the Supreme Court—*Roe v. Wade* and *Doe v. Bolton*—arrived in 1973. Both dealt with the constitutionality of two state laws that placed restrictions on a woman's right to have an abortion. The Roe case (Roe was a fictitious name, as was Doe, to safeguard the privacy of the woman in the matter) concerned a Texas statute that made it a felony to destroy a fetus unless doctors said the abortion was necessary to save the mother's life. The Doe case involved a Georgia law that allowed an abortion only in three instances—when the mother's health was threatened, when the pregnancy resulted from a rape, or when the expected child would be born with a severe mental or physical handicap.

The Court, using both the Fourteenth and Ninth Amendments to reach a decision, came out in favor of a woman's right to choose freely to have an abortion and declared both laws unconstitutional by 7–2 votes. Justice Harry Blackmun wrote the opinion for the Court. He pointed out that the constitutional right to privacy is seen in the concept of personal liberty as voiced in the Fourteenth Amendment and in the unspecified rights that are held by the people via the Ninth Amendment. That right to privacy, he continued, "includes the right of a woman to decide whether or not to terminate her pregnancy."

But Justice Blackmun went on to write that the right to have an abortion is not an "unqualified" right. The states, he remarked, have an interest in regulating abortions for the public good and it is an interest that must be recognized. He then outlined what a state might and might not do in regulating abortions.

First, during the opening trimester of pregnancy (the first three months) a state may not prohibit abortions but is permitted to regulate the procedure to protect the mother's health. In the next months, the state may regulate certain matters; it may, for instance, set standards to be observed in performing abortions and establish regulations concerning who can perform them and where they can be performed. It may also deny a woman an abortion if medical opinion advises against it and has the right to do so when the unborn child becomes "viable"—able to survive outside the mother's womb. In general, a fetus is considered viable in the final trimester, the last three months of pregnancy.

The Supreme Court's decision in the two cases legalized abortion in the United States and triggered a controversy between those in favor of the procedure on the grounds of freedom of choice for the woman, and those who oppose it on moral grounds. The controversy rages to this day.

Though the cases involving abortion and private sexual practices have captured the greatest public attention, the Court has also issued decisions on such privacy matters as wiretapping and the dividing line between illegal and legal searches and seizures. These decisions, along with all the judge-made and statute laws that we've mentioned in this chapter, are now to play a major role in the coming pages as we look at the steps you can take to protect yourself when the world gets too nosy for comfort.

CHAPTER FOUR

PRIVACY AND YOUR HOME

The home has long been called the family's castle, the fortress where the family has its greatest right, in the words of Louis Brandeis, "to be let alone." But, unfortunately, it is a fortress that is vulnerable to all sorts of attacks—trespass, illegal searches and seizures, and floods of unwanted mail and telephone calls.

You may think that these assaults have little to do with you as a young person. You're right. But they are attacks that you may well encounter in the future. It's best to begin arming yourself now with the knowledge that will be needed to handle them properly should they ever crop up in your life.

In addition, we're going to turn to a problem that you've likely run into already as a young person—the ways in which the members of the family violate one another's privacy. We'll look at what can be done to make certain that everyone in your house enjoys the greatest amount of privacy possible.

TRESPASS

Trespass occurs when someone enters your property without your permission, either express or implied. Express permission is given when you invite someone to come to your house for a social or business reason. Implied permission is given to anyone who has your unspoken invitation to come onto the property—for example, delivery people and neighbors or friends who drop by for a visit. You'll recall from Chapter Three that virtually all our states have statutes describing and prohibiting trespass.

Though your right to privacy is violated by trespass, your right here is not absolute. When faced with a trespasser, you must always remember that he has certain rights as a human being, even though he is committing an illegal act. The law requires that you respect those rights. If you don't, the trespasser will be able to bring a lawsuit against you for any harm he suffers during the trespass.

The first of your rights has to do with the condition in which you keep your property. Since the trespasser is entering your property without invitation, he is doing so at his own risk. And so you have the right *not* to keep your property safe for him. This means that you need not remove any potentially dangerous obstacles in his path if they are normal parts of the property.

Suppose that a trespasser—we'll call him Al—sneaks into your front yard one night and breaks his leg when he trips over the rocks that serve as a decorative border for the walkway leading to your porch. He cannot bring suit for his broken leg. Nor can he complain should he tumble into a ditch or walk into a low-hanging tree branch and blacken his eye. These hazards are the kind that are normally found on private properties.

Now when do Al's rights take over? While you need not keep your property safe for his forays, you do not have the right to set traps for him. Suppose that a stone wall surrounds your property. When Al tries to climb over it, he cuts himself on chunks of broken glass that you've had embedded there in concrete. This is a dangerous trap. He is entitled to sue you for his injuries.

The same holds true if you dot your property with such snares as bear traps, camouflaged pits, and guns set to discharge when Al trips over a wire stretched across his path. The same also holds true if you keep vicious dogs that are trained to attack intruders.

When Al invades your property, you have every right to eject him. But you must take care in how you do so. You must use what the law calls the "least adequate" degree of force. This "least adequate" degree will depend on the circumstances. It can range all the way from injuring or killing Al to simply showing him the way back to your front gate.

For example, let's say that, when you catch sight of Al, he comes at you with his fists, a club, or a gun. You are entitled to knock him down, render him unconscious, or perhaps even kill him if that is the only way you can adequately defend yourself. But, once you have stopped his attack or have sent him running, you must end your defense. If you've knocked him senseless, for instance, you may not continue to beat him out of revenge or anger.

Should Al be the innocent type of trespasser—the sort who can be shooed off with a shout or will depart as soon as you tell him he is trespassing—you may use little or no force at all. You may not fire a shotgun at him, set your dog loose on him, or chase after him, swinging a club or cane and striking him with it.

In addition to these rules, there are two others that you must remember. First, the rule that you need not keep your property in safe condition for trespassers no longer applies when you do nothing to stop people from frequently or regularly trespassing on your land. Suppose that children constantly use a portion of your property as a shortcut to school and that you've never warned them to stop. Your failure to warn them off means that you've given them your implied permission to use the shortcut, and you must now exercise reasonable care in seeing that they are not injured while using it. For instance, should they routinely cross your private roadway at a certain point, you are required always to drive with extra caution when you approach the spot.

Second, your property should not have on it what is called an "attractive nuisance." This is some feature or condition that is obviously inviting to children, is a danger to them, and that they, by virtue of their age, do not recognize as hazardous. A swampy area, a swimming pool, a stand of trees that beg to be climbed—all qualify as attractive nuisances. You can be sued for any injury they cause if you do not take adequate steps to safeguard children from them.

To protect yourself against damage suits by trespassers, you should post your property with signs warning that trespassing is forbidden. The signs, of course, should be done in large, easy-to-read print and should be placed where they can be readily seen.

SEARCH AND SEIZURE

As you'll recall from Chapter Two, our Founding Fathers, thanks to years of experience with a harsh British rule, were painfully aware of how intrusive a government can be when they wrote the Bill of Rights. As a result, they placed in it the Fourth Amendment, which made the home safe from unreasonable searches and seizures. But their use of the word "unreasonable" left the way open for the authorities to conduct reasonable—and thus, legal—searches and seizures.

For a search of your home and/or the seizure of goods within it to be reasonable, the authorities must abide by certain rules prior to knocking on your door. They must obtain a search warrant from the court. The court (meaning here, a judge) is not to issue the warrant unless convinced that there is good reason to enter the home. In legal terms, the authorities must show him that there is "probable cause" for their suspicions, meaning that they must demonstrate to the judge that the search will actually uncover a crime, a criminal, or evidence of a crime, and not be a "fishing expedition" that merely hopes to find something wrong.

If the entry is to be made for the purpose of apprehending a criminal suspect, the authorities will ask the court for an arrest warrant. But, before it is issued, probable cause for the coming arrest must be shown.

For a search or an arrest warrant to be legal, it must specify:

- The exact place to be searched
- The purpose of the search

- The person or things to be seized
- The date on which the warrant is issued and the length of time it is to remain in effect

When the authorities arrive at your door, you have the right to demand to see their search or arrest warrant. If they do not have it in hand, you have the right to refuse them entry and to tell them to return with a warrant, at which time you'll be willing to cooperate with them.

There are certain instances, however, in which a warrant is not required before a home can be entered. They are meant to enable the authorities to do their job in a number of situations that pose a threat to the householder or the public. For one, when the police are pursuing a criminal and see him enter a private home, they may immediately follow him inside. They may also enter if they believe that any criminal evidence to be found inside will be destroyed in the time it takes to obtain a warrant. And, of course, they may enter without a warrant in the event of an emergency—such as a fire or the known presence of an armed person who is holding the people inside hostage and threatening their lives.

Should the authorities manage to enter your home without a warrant or without meeting any of the above conditions for a warrantless search, they will have conducted an illegal search and seizure. More than a quarter of a century ago, the U.S. Supreme Court ruled that the evidence collected in such an entry may not be then used in a court trial.

We need here to mention another of your possessions that

is more likely than your home to be the subject of a search one day—your automobile. It is not afforded the same protections that are granted to the home. Suppose the police stop you for a traffic violation and catch sight of something illegal next to you on the front seat—perhaps a handgun or a plastic package of powder that looks suspiciously like cocaine. They have the right to search the car immediately. (And you may be certain that they'll glance into the car's interior on approaching it; they'll do so to protect themselves against the possibility that you have a weapon of some sort in your possession.) All they need is probable cause to believe that the car contains something illegal or dangerous to conduct a search on the spot. In great part, they are given these freedoms because a car can be easily driven away with potentially incriminating evidence.

YOUR MAILBOX

There's hardly a one of us who hasn't had our fair share of "junk mail"—all those uninvited advertisements, catalogs, and appeals for charitable contributions that arrive in our mailboxes, sometimes daily, from direct mailing companies. Journalist Jeffrey Rothfeder, in his book, *Privacy for Sale: How Computerization Has Made Everyone's Private Life an Open Secret*, writes that we Americans receive no fewer than a staggering 63 billion pieces of junk mail each year. The U.S. Postal Service reports that over 38 percent of its annual revenues comes from the handling of junk mail.

Many of us are quite happy to receive junk mail. For some, especially the elderly, it is the only mail they receive. Others welcome certain of the advertisements and catalogs and make their purchases from them. Still others are complimented by the amount of junk mail that lands on their doorstep. They see it as a sign that they're known as people prosperous enough to afford what the mailers have to sell.

The sending of junk mail is not illegal and is not, in itself, an invasion of our privacy. What angers us—and strikes us as a privacy violation—is the business of gathering the necessary information on us and then peddling it to companies that can profit from it. But what can you do to stem the tide of junk mail—either because you dislike it or want to fight back against all the information gathering that lurks behind it? Here are some suggestions:

Journalist Frances Leonard, in a recent issue of *Modern Maturity* magazine, advises that you write to the Direct Marketing Association, an organization that represents companies in the direct mail business, and request to have your name deleted from the lists of its client firms. The Association, she explains, can remove your name from most nationally distributed lists. Address your letter to the Association's Mail Preference Service and include your full name, address, and zip code. The Association's address is P.O. Box 3861, New York, New York 10163-3861.

When you renew a magazine subscription or make a purchase from a mail-order catalog, Leonard advises you to specify that your name not be made available to other companies.

You can also write directly to the companies that are sending you advertisements and catalogs and request that they dispense with your name. They are not required to honor your request, but many will make the effort to do so.

Finally, you can refuse to buy anything from any company that fails to honor your request. After a time, your refusal to buy may cause some of the companies, when updating their mailing lists, to drop your name. Well-run direct-mail firms are not interested in wasting printing costs and postage on "nonbuying" customers.

YOUR TELEPHONE

There is no doubt that the telephone is one of the greatest technological miracles of all time. It enables us, customarily in a matter of seconds, to talk with people in all parts of the world. But, in the minds of millions of Americans, there is also no doubt that it has become the world's most intrusive instrument.

Consider how it has intruded on life in your home. Have you ever been playing some kind of table game with your family, only to have the phone ring and put an end to the fun for long minutes while your mother or someone else took the call? And, when your older sister has been helping you with your homework, hasn't she been summoned to the phone for a chat with a friend more times than not? In these cases—and in many another that you can think of—the odds are that the answer to the questions is an annoyed "yes."

And, of course, in this day and age of telemarketing, you've certainly seen your mother or father called away from the dinner table to sigh with impatience when the caller at the other end of the line has something to sell. Research shows that each day sees more than 18 million Americans receive telemarketing calls.

Just what can you do to keep the telephone from intruding so often on your privacy? Let's start with your friends and relatives. There are those among them whose calls are always welcome. But there are those who have the knack for calling at exactly the wrong time—just as you're sitting down to dinner or to your homework. Why not gently and politely let them know when the best times are to call? A few may be annoyed (hopefully, for just a short while), but most will understand and appreciate your desire or need not to be disturbed at certain times.

You can also buy an inexpensive telephone-answering machine that asks the caller to leave a recorded message. Whenever the phone rings, just let it jangle until the machine clicks in. When you learn who is on the other end of the line, you can call back at a convenient time. The machine will also screen telemarketing sales calls. In fact, it will cause such callers to hang up immediately and move on to their next numbers.

Depending on where you live, you might be able to fit your telephone with what is called "Caller I.D." Presently available to phone customers in upwards of twenty states and under consideration for use in some others, it is a service that places a small electronic screen alongside your telephone. Whenever the phone rings, the number of the caller appears on the screen, giving you the choice of answering or ignoring the call. The service usually costs around $6 to $7 a month, plus a charge that can range from $45 to about $85 for the installation of the screen.

Ever since it became available, Caller I.D. has triggered

both praise and criticism. On the one hand, many people look on it as a fine protection against annoying calls and a way of fighting obscene calls. Delivery businesses, such as pizza shops, fast-food restaurants, and florists, see it as a convenience that enables them to check that incoming orders are valid and not pranks.

On the other hand, it is criticized as a threat to the privacy of the callers. For instance, some companies use Caller I.D. to display the number of anyone who calls with questions about their products or services. The companies can then use the number to obtain further information about the customer from a computer data base. The police worry that many people will be reluctant to call with anonymous tips on criminal activities if they think that Caller I.D. will deprive them of their anonymity. The same holds true for people who call anonymously to receive information or help from drug abuse, child abuse, alcohol abuse, or runaway hot lines.

If Caller I.D. is not available in your state or if you'd prefer to use a modified version of it, your telephone company may be able to provide you with the service known generally as "Call Screen." This service enables you to block out several numbers from which you don't wish to receive calls. Usually, you can block out up to ten such numbers. You do so by entering a simple code in your telephone and following it with the numbers to be blocked. There is usually a monthly fee of a few dollars for the service.

If you're being bothered by obscene or other offending calls, you might want to look into a new service that a number of telephone companies are offering to end the problem. Generally known as "Call Trace," it enables you to dial

44

a special code after hanging up, at which time the telephone company will record the number from which the call originated. The information will be released to the law enforcement agency that investigates such calls. The telephone company will not release a traced number to any customer, not even to you. There is a charge for the service. It may vary from state to state. Some companies, among them Pacific Bell of California, do not require a monthly fee for the service, but charge for each call traced. Such a charge may range up to $5 per call, rising to a maximum of perhaps $25 a month.

Now, what steps can you take to reduce the number of telemarketing calls?

As can be done in the case of unwanted junk mail, you can write to the Direct Marketing Association, which represents telemarketers as well as direct mailers. This time, include your phone number and area code. Your letter should be addressed to the Association's Telephone Preference Service.

You might also tell all telemarketing callers that you're not interested in buying anything and that you want your name and number taken off their lists. Depending on the callers and the company they represent, this tactic may not work, but it's worth a try.

Many telemarketing firms do not work only with purchased lists. They develop their own lists, gathering them from local telephone directories. And so you may want to have your number unlisted in your local directory. In most states, a small monthly fee, usually no more than a few cents, is charged for this service. You should be warned, however, that your unlisted name and number may not remain a secret. It's long been common practice for telephone companies to make their unlisted numbers available to various governmental agencies to assist them in their work. Among the recipients are police forces, the Federal Bureau of Investigation, county welfare and health departments, and the armed services.

And now a tip on protecting yourself against one of the ugliest telephone tricks:

You may receive a call one day from someone who tells you that you've just won a new car or a vacation trip in a contest you've never heard of. The caller says that he needs some information to determine that you are indeed the winner and then asks for your credit card number or the name of your bank. Hang up. He's looking for information that is going to land you on someone's mailing list or he's setting you up for some sort of trickery—perhaps the use of your credit card number to make purchases with it over the phone.

In addition to the above points, there are some things that should be kept in mind about your privacy whenever you use the telephone.

To begin, most of us believe that the telephone is a very private instrument and that our conversations cannot be overheard by others. Such was not always the case. There was a time when many phones were on "party lines," meaning that a number of people all shared the same line and could listen in on one another's conversations if they so chose. While there are some party lines still in operation, especially in rural areas, most telephones today are linked to single households. This has caused many people to trust that their conversations on it are strictly private.

Their trust is misplaced. Every phone conversation can be—and many often are—monitored by others. The law permits telephone companies to listen in on calls to check the quality of their service; millions of such checks are made annually. Likewise, companies whose employees deal with customers over the phone are permitted to "tune in" to learn if the employees' politeness is up to par. Over the years, countless telephone conversations have been monitored and/or recorded for a wide variety of other reasons.

The monitoring and/or recording of telephone calls is known as "wiretapping." The term refers to the use of electronic devices to eavesdrop on conversations that are carried over a wire. There are a host of such devices—microphones and recorders of various sizes, transmitters, and antennae. When the same or similar devices are used to intercept conversations not carried over a wire—conversations in a home, hotel room, or car, for instance—they are called "bugs," with the interceptions themselves known as "bugging."

Wiretapping dates back to the first days of the telephone in the late 1880s. For many years, the wiretapping of suspected and known criminals to gain the evidence needed to convict them was deemed legal. Then, in a series of cases during the 1960s, the U.S. Supreme Court delared that telephone and other private conversations are protected under the Fourth and Fifth Amendments—under the Fourth because secret wiretapping and bugging amount to unreasonable searches, and under the Fifth because they can lead the unwary victims to give evidence against themselves. Next, Congress in 1968, in reply to a growing public concern over the mushrooming of crime and violence in the nation, enacted the Omnibus Crime Control and Safe Streets Act. One of its provisions made both wiretapping and bugging crimes.

In general, both actions have been illegal ever since, unless carried out with a court order, which is the equivalent of a search warrant. As in the case of search warrants, the authorities may not record or otherwise eavesdrop on someone's conversation by wiretap or bug unless they can show the court that there is ample reason to suspect that someone of criminal or subversive activities. There are also a number of exceptions to the Omnibus Crime Control Act's provisions. The president is allowed to authorize wiretaps and bugs in any case that he deems a threat to the country's security. The U.S. attorney general may give permission for wiretaps and bugs in cases involving major federal felonies, such as kidnapping, murder, treason, espionage, counterfeiting, and drug-related crimes. The Act also allows state attorneys general, judges, and district attorneys to sanction wiretaps and bugs in cases in which serious infractions of state laws are suspected.

You may think that the Supreme Court's decisions in the 1960s and the Omnibus Crime and Safe Streets Act make your telephone conversations safe from being monitored and recorded. If so, you're mistaken. Remember, the law still gives telephone companies and employers the right to monitor calls. Further, the Omnibus Crime Control Act and the laws in most states make it legal to record a telephone conversation when one party or the other agrees to the recording; still further, the party who is doing the recording need not inform the other party of what is happening. What it adds up to is this: you may call Jack on the telephone and record the conversation without his knowledge. What you may not do is somehow hook into his line and record his conversation with someone else. Nor may you record the conversations of others in your own home if they are using your phone extensions. (A few states, California among them, say that recordings cannot be made unless both parties agree to them.)

While the law gives you much protection against wiretapping and bugging, you must remember that not all people adhere to the law. Companies wiretap and bug other companies to learn their secret product developments. Husbands and wives turn to wiretapping and bugging to discover if their spouses are being unfaithful to them. The possibility that you may one day have your phone conversations overheard and recorded without your knowledge should mean just one thing to you: always be careful of what you say.

PRIVACY AND YOUR FAMILY

Privacy can be a pretty hard thing to come by in family living. It's so easy to have your own privacy disturbed or for you to disturb someone else's privacy. Little brothers and sisters have the bad habit of barging into the bathroom when you're using it—or of banging on the door just as you're combing your hair or checking out your complexion. Your mother routinely goes through your pockets before putting your slacks or skirt into the washer, always with the risk of stumbling upon something you don't want her to see—perhaps a forbidden pack of cigarettes or a note from that special someone in your life.

Everyone wants some degree of privacy, with some desiring a great deal of privacy, and some just a little. You've likely already noticed that one brother or sister likes to be alone much of the time while another loves to be surrounded by the whole family. And you've probably noticed that some family members don't like to share their private thoughts, while others are willing to tell all about themselves to anyone willing to listen.

Regardless of the degree needed, the want for privacy is still there, continually or at one time or another, in every family member. Every effort should be made to respect that desire.

As a young person today and later as an adult with children of your own, you can take a number of steps to honor the privacy of your family members.

For one, suppose that you share a room with a brother or sister. Arrange things so that certain areas of the room belong to one or the other of you. Let each of you have a bureau, desk drawers, or even a box for your own personal possessions. Then make certain that neither of you noses into the other's space and possessions. The room may be small, but these arrangements can give each of you a definite sense of privacy.

If you accidentally come upon a secret possession of a family member, leave it alone. Perhaps your sister forgets to lock her diary away after making an entry in it. Should you see it, don't give in to the temptation of reading what she's written. Should the temptation prove too great, then forget what you've read. Above all else, don't mention what you've seen to anyone else, even if you think it's hilarious. And don't make fun of your sister for her secret revelations. If you fail to do any of these things, you'll be embarrassing and hurting her—and violating her privacy.

The fact is that the privacy that is granted to young people in the home is more of a privilege than a right. Your mother is granting you the privilege of privacy when she finds those forbidden cigarettes in your clothing and then speaks quietly to you about them rather than broadcasting the news to the rest of the family. Your brother and sister are granting you the privilege of privacy when they don't pick up an extension phone and listen in on your conversations. They're granting you the privilege of privacy when, knowing that noise makes you nervous, they keep their stereo sets turned down when you're around.

The family members who grant you these privileges—and so many others—all share one characteristic in common: a sympathy for and a consideration of your feelings. That sympathy and consideration can serve as the keystones for solving all privacy problems, not only in the home but everywhere else—in school, at work, in any public place, and among friends and relatives. With it, everyone greets with kindness your need and desire for privacy while you make certain that you greet with kindness their very same need and desire.

CHAPTER FIVE

PRIVACY AND YOUR SCHOOL

If your formal education began with nursery school or kindergarten, you'll spend about fourteen years in the classroom before receiving your high school diploma. During those years, you'll be in the hands of teachers and administrators who are granted a great deal of authority over you.

They hold this authority because, in the eyes of the law, they stand *in loco parentis* while you are in their charge. The term means that they stand in place of your parents and, as a result, have much the same powers as your mother and father. It is their right—and duty—to see that you obey all school rules, that you act and study in ways deemed necessary for the successful pursuit of your education, and that you behave in no way that hinders them in performing their jobs properly.

THREE MATTERS OF PRIVACY

The authority granted to teachers and administrators extends to matters that many people, young and old alike, consider to be highly private. We begin with three that may be troubling you at present. After talking briefly about them, we'll turn to a matter that, in this age of information gathering and distribution, can be a major problem for you, not only today but in the years to come—the handling of your school records.

Matter #1: Dress and Hairstyle

Just about every student thinks that his or her choice of clothing and hairstyle is a personal matter and is no one else's business. But, in fact, it is the school's business. Though you may protest that your privacy is being invaded, your school has the right to govern your dress and hairstyle unless prohibited from doing so by school district policy or a local law. But don't go searching for such a law if your principal hates your jeans or hairdo. Hardly any community has one.

Your school has the right to set a code that it thinks will result in a tasteful student appearance. The code is meant to insure that clothing and hairstyles will not cause problems on campus or hamper the educational process.

Many school districts allow each of their schools to establish its own dress and hair code. Often, to keep the students happy and to acknowledge their individuality, a school will opt for a code that is in keeping with current fashions for young people. Some schools set their codes according to the prevailing attitudes in their communities. The codes will be strict in those communities that insist on a certain standard of dress for their young people. They'll be liberal in communities that believe it is the right of students to express their individuality by wearing what they wish.

If you object to your school's dress code, there is really only one thing you can do about it. You can marshal as many students and parents as possible and approach the district board with the request to revise or drop the code. The board may honor your request, but is in no way required to.

A private or parochial school is better able than a public school to establish a strict dress code. This is because the student seeks enrollment there and must, if he or she wishes to be accepted, obey its dress code.

Many educators believe there is a strong link between the way students dress and the way they work. Simply put, the feeling is that sloppy dress produces sloppy study and classroom habits, while neat dress produces the exact opposite result. This belief is currently gaining favor in a growing number of school districts, whose codes are now requiring conservative dress or a uniformlike clothing, such as identical slacks and sweaters for the boys and identical skirts and sweaters for the girls.

Matter #2: Morals, Health, and Safety

Teachers and administrators have the right and the duty to look into any matter that poses a threat to your moral well-being, health, and safety, and then to take whatever action is needed to correct the problem, including the handing out of punishment.

The right to check and act is not limited to the classroom; it can be exercised anywhere on the campus. If you're a boy, you may think that a fight with your worst enemy out in a far corner of the football field is a private matter between the two of you. Not so. The health of two students is endangered and every faculty and staff member is empowered and required to put a stop to the fracas and do whatever is necessary to restore peace.

Nor is the right limited to the hours when class is in session. It can be exercised at sporting events, rallies, dances, and all other school activities. Nor is it limited to the school premises, but is extended to any off-campus event in which the school is participating, as you'll learn if you're discovered and then disciplined for sneaking a beer with your date during the senior prom at a local hotel.

Where does the right end? In general, the laws hold that it ends once you're back home or are otherwise under the control of your parents. Should you then pull some dumb stunt that can be called an ordinary act of misbehavior— say, toss a rock at your neighbor's window or tie a tin can to his cat's tail—the school authorities will have no right to punish you. That job will belong to your parents.

The law, however, grants your school some control over you while you are on your way to and from the campus. It has the right to discipline you should you behave in a way harmful to the best interests of the school or your fellow students. Suppose that, as you're walking home, you talk a friend into skipping class the next day so that you can go to the beach. You're in trouble if one of your teachers learns of what you've done. The school also has the right and the duty to take whatever steps are necessary to put an end to any criminal activities in which you may be involved, whether at home or on or off-campus, such as shoplifting, car theft, or drug dealing.

There is one family matter that the laws of every state require the schools to report—child abuse. Should your teachers learn or come to suspect that you or another student is bruised and cut due to abuse at home, they must report the problem to the authorities for investigation. Their failure to do so will leave them open to criminal action—usually on misdemeanor charges—and may see them fined or jailed. The laws, however, protect them in lawsuits by the family should the reports prove to be groundless. All that is required is that the reports be made in good faith.

Such reports were not required at one time because child abuse—which is far more cruel than ordinary punishments—was often mistakenly seen as necessary for the disciplining of some children. As such, it was regarded as a private family matter. But the recent years, which have brought an increase in child abuses because of such factors as the stresses of everyday life, have also brought a public change of mind and, as a result, the reporting laws. The mistreatment of children is no longer viewed as a private family matter but as the business of the entire community. Required to make the reports are not only teachers, but also doctors and nurses, attorneys, social workers, police officers, and public officials.

Matter #3: Locker Searches

The matter of whether the police or the school authorities have the right to search your locker without your consent or a warrant has long been a source of argument. The problem has centered on the question of who actually owns the locker—you or the school district. Some people have argued that the locker is yours—or, at the least, contains your property—and so is protected against warrantless searches by the Fourth Amendment. But others have held that it belongs to the school district and is on loan to you. Hence, it is the district's property and can be searched without your permission.

In general, the law today agrees with the view that the locker belongs to the district. It can be searched by the school authorities themselves without your permission, and by the police if given permission to do so by the school principal. The principal is entitled to give this permission not only because the locker is school property but also because he stands *in loco parentis* while you are in his charge. However, many, if not most, school districts exercise common sense when deciding whether a locker should be searched, attempting the searches only when they feel there is reason to suspect that it contains such items as stolen goods, drugs, or weapons.

YOUR SCHOOL RECORDS

Now we come to the matter that can prove worrisome not only at present but also throughout your entire academic life and even into the years following your high school or college graduation.

Along with many another student, you may think that your school records contain no more than the names of the schools you've attended and the grades you've earned in class. If so, you're in for a major shock the first time you take a look at them.

Records of your school career are kept from the very first day you attend your first class. They contain your grades, yes, but can also hold a staggering amount of additional information—medical data; the results of psychological, personality, and IQ testing; the comments of teachers, counselors, and administrators on your behavior, character, and aptitudes (or lack of them); and even notes on what you've had to say in interviews with counselors—your answers to questions about such personal matters as your views of your parents, your sexual activities, and your possible use of drugs.

The records follow you throughout your elementary and high school years and then move on to college with you. They play a part in your acceptance or rejection by a new school or by a university you wish to attend. They may even follow you into your early adulthood when you go in search of your first job. In all, they are meant to help a number of people who are unacquainted with you—teachers, administrators, and prospective employers—decide whether they want to have anything to do with you.

The records can pose a problem for any student. This is because they can contain material of a detrimental nature— uncomplimentary opinions by teachers and administrators that may be in error or that no longer apply.

Robert Ellis Smith, in *Privacy: How to Protect What's Left of It*, gives three examples of teacher opinions so mistaken that they are hilarious. The first of the trio was voiced in the nineteenth century; it branded a young boy as "retarded" and caused him to be expelled from school. The second comes to us from the eighteenth century and held that a young music student had no talent whatsoever as a composer. Finally, in the seventeenth century, there was a teacher's judgment that an elementary-age boy was a hopelessly poor pupil.

The three youngsters were, in turn, Thomas Alva Edison (1847–1931), who gave us the electric light and patented

more than 1,000 inventions in his lifetime; Ludwig van Bee-
thoven (1770–1827), who is revered as one of the world's
greatest composers of classical music; and Isaac Newton
(1643–1727), the "poor" student who made major contributions to mathematics and science and explained the laws
of motion and universal gravitation.

Now, what of information that no longer applies? A few
years ago, a high school sophomore wanted to transfer to
a private school and was surprised when he was refused.
He knew that his grades were good enough to win him
admission. His mother, wondering if his school records
might contain some damaging entries, asked to see them.
She came upon a notation from the private school that her
son was unacceptable because he was a known troublemaker. The decision was made on the basis of a teacher's
comments on his unruly behavior back in the third grade.
The boy had been emotionally upset over the fact that his
parents were divorcing. Once he worked his way through
his problem, all was well. There were no further comments
on misbehavior in the classroom. Yet, the private school had
failed to take this into account and had reacted to a single,
long out-of-date teacher opinion.

Because the records are so important to a student's academic career and because they can contain errors and faulty
opinions, parents and students have long wanted to be able
to check them for content and accuracy. Prior to 1974, there
was no law that enabled them to do so. The situation was
an odd one. The records could be—and were—made available to many agencies, among them police departments,
newspapers, prospective employers, schools and colleges
considering the student for admission, and the armed ser-

vices. But not to the parents and students themselves—not unless the school consented to make them available.

All this changed in the summer of 1974, when Congress enacted the Family Educational Rights and Privacy Act.

The Family Educational Rights and Privacy Act

The Act, which is popularly known as the Buckley Amendment in honor of its sponsor, former New York Senator James L. Buckley, gives you or your parents the right to review your records if your school is supported by federal funds. It provides that:

You yourself have the right to see your school records if you are eighteen years of age or older. If you have yet to reach your eighteenth birthday, the right belongs to your parents. They must, however, have your permission before exercising this right.

The school may not charge a fee for making the records available for review.

You (or your parents) may make copies of the records or make notes for personal use and later reference. However, the records may not be taken home. All copying and note-taking must be done at the school.

You (or, again, your parents) are entitled to ask that inaccuracies and misstatements in the records be changed. In order to have the records altered, you are permitted to meet with and explain your objections to the school authorities. If they refuse to act on your complaint, you are then entitled to attach a personal statement to the records, explaining your disagreement with what they have to say. The statement is then to be made a permanent part of the records and is to accompany them wherever they go.

If you believe that your rights under the Act are being violated or disregarded by the school authorities, you have the right to lodge a complaint with the federal government by writing to the U.S. Department of Education, 400 Maryland Avenue, S.W., Washington, D.C. 20202.

In addition to the rights that it grants to you or your parents, the Act limits the school's ability to make your records available to outside parties. It states that federal funds will not go to any school or college with the policy or practice of releasing educational records without the written consent of the student or the parents. But there are exceptions to this rule that enable the records to be distributed to certain parties without consent. More about the exceptions in a moment.

The Act has been of help to many students and their parents. But it has failed to please just as many others. Ever since its passage, it has been the target of a variety of complaints.

For one, the Act is widely criticized for not granting the right of review to *every* student and parent in the nation. The Act covers only public schools and colleges that receive federal support. It does not apply to parochial and private schools. If you attend one or the other and wish to see your records, you'll have to depend on the cooperation of its principal and teachers.

Next, though the Act requires that the written consent of the student or the parents be obtained before a school makes the records available to some parties, it does allow distribution without consent to a wide variety of individuals and agencies. Among them are school officials in your district and elsewhere; schools or colleges that you hope to attend; organizations that provide student loans and other types of educational aid; and educational testing and research services.

The individuals and agencies to which the records can be sent without consent customarily need them for their work. The fear that your privacy rights will be violated here centers on the fact that the Act does not limit what the recipients can then do with the records. They may provide them to others, making your academic records known to an ever-widening circle of organizations and individuals.

Especially bothersome to many people is the fact that the Act allows a school or university to ask that you sign an agreement not to demand a look at certain of your records. You'll likely run up against this agreement—called a waiver—when you're in college and would like to see what the people who wrote letters of recommendation on your behalf had to say about you. The Act permits the school or college to ask for the waiver to protect the privacy of the letter writers. The belief is that many teachers and others will be reluctant to write candidly and honestly about you if they know that, sooner or later, you're apt to see what they've written.

Schools and colleges have the right to ask for your signature on the waiver, but not the right to insist on it. Nor, if you're applying for admittance, do they have right to turn you down if you put up a squawk. Further, no school or college may ask you to waive your rights in general when you request a look at your records.

Most students end up signing the waiver. They commonly think that they'll harm their educational careers or their chances of being admitted to the institution of their choice if they do otherwise. They may also think that their refusal will cause the school or college to look on them as troublemakers.

If you sign the waiver, you may limit it to the present, while saying that you want to retain the right to see the letters at some time in the future. If you decide on this route, you should attach a letter explaining your reasons for wanting to check them later on. Robert Ellis Smith suggests several reasons that can be mentioned in the letter. Among them are: your wish to see that the information in the letters is correct; your desire to learn what the letter writers think to be your strengths and weaknesses so that you can take steps to improve them; and your desire to learn if any of the letter writers think enough of you to write another letter on your behalf at some future date, perhaps when you go in search of a job.

CHAPTER SIX

PRIVACY AND YOUR JOB:
When You Enter the Workplace

If you think your school is threatening your privacy too much, wait until you enter the workplace. Unless you are very fortunate in your choice of an employer, your right to privacy is going to be challenged in numerous ways, especially if you land a job in what is called the private sector.

TWO SECTORS AND A WORLD OF DIFFERENCE

When you go to work, you will be employed in either the private or the public sector. The first, as its name indicates, is made up of private companies and business firms. Found in the latter are all the people who work for governmental bodies—local, state, and federal.

The two sectors differ greatly in the rights granted to you as an employee. But the two are alike in one way. Various federal and state laws prohibit both public- and private-sector employers from firing or refusing to hire you (or thwarting your advancement on the job) for such reasons as your race, religion, national origin, and age. To defy these prohibitions is to discriminate against you.

The major difference between the two sectors is seen in the protection of your constitutional rights. Those rights are well protected in the public sector. Safeguarding them, first of all, are certain of the amendments to the Constitution. Your right to privacy as an employee, for instance, is protected by the Fourth and Fifth Amendments because they are directed against intrusions by governmental bodies and thus apply to your employer. In another area, the Fifth and Fourteenth Amendments protect you from any government action that deprives you of the right to "life, liberty or property without due process of law"; for you as a government worker, this means that your employer may not discipline or fire you without a reasonable cause having to do with job performance. Further protections are provided by an assortment of federal and state laws and by the Civil Service rules that regulate the employment of public workers from the local to the national level.

Things are different in the private sector. As a private worker, you do not share the public worker's protection against being unjustly fired. Why is this so? The American Civil Liberties Union (ACLU), the national organization that is dedicated to protecting the constitutional rights of all U.S. citizens, provides the answer by saying that American private business functions under the doctrine known as "employment at will." The doctrine, which the ACLU describes as a leftover from the antilabor laws of the nineteenth century, gives employers the right to discharge workers for any reason, no matter whether justifed or not.

The doctrine of "employment at will" and the power to fire for any reason also enable private employers to suppress certain rights that the worker should be able to enjoy. One such right that is known to have been suppressed at times is the right of free expression—as witness the Pennsylvania worker who was discharged some years ago after speaking out against the serious safety defects in his company's product.

Nor are there any federal or state laws that prohibit private employers and companies from disciplining or firing you without just cause or from violating your privacy, as an Indiana woman learned some years ago when she was fired not for inefficiency on the job but because her cigarette-hating boss learned that she smoked in her home.

Whatever protections you enjoy as a private-sector worker have come from other directions. They've been awarded to you by a sensible employer; you've won them on your own by proving your worth; or they've been obtained by your labor union in its contract agreements with your employer. Practically all union contracts stipulate that union workers can be fired only for adequate cause and only after a hearing before a neutral arbitrator.

Thankfully, however, there are a few federal and state employment laws that do provide some safeguards for your privacy in the private sector. At the federal level, there is the Employee Polygraph Protection Act (EPPA), which Congress enacted in 1988; it keeps many private companies and business firms from requiring job applicants and employees to take lie detector tests. Some states have also enacted laws against the urine testing that is meant to detect the presence of drugs in employees. Both the lie detector test and the urine test have caused such widespread outrage in the work-place and are considered such threats to privacy that they are the subjects of Chapter Seven.

Aside from the restrictions imposed by these few laws, virtually all of the rights in the private sector belong to the employers. Employers have the right to expect a full and honest day's work from you. They have the right to set performance and safety standards and to expect you to meet them. They have the right to expect that you will have your wits about you while on the job—that you won't be drunk, too tired to function properly, or under the influence of drugs. Should you violate any of these rights, you give your employer just cause to discipline or even fire you.

The private-sector employer holds these rights because they enable a company to perform efficiently, protect the quality of its product, help to insure the safety of your fellow workers, and assure the company that your salary is money well spent. But, in the pursuit of these aims, many private employers overstep their bounds and poke their noses into your personal business—and poke deeply at times. The trouble can begin on the day you begin looking for work.

APPLYING FOR A JOB

When you apply for a job, you can count on being asked a long string of personal questions. They begin with the job application. You should be prepared to answer inquiries ranging from the most innocent to the nosiest. Here are a few examples (some of which you'll also encounter in the public sector):

- What is your Social Security number?

- What is your age?

- What is your driver's license number? When does your license expire?

- Who should be informed in the event you are injured on the job?

- Are you married, single, divorced, or widowed? If single, are you engaged to be married?

- What is your father's income?

You may be among the many applicants who object to certain of these questions. You may wonder why you're being asked at this time for your Social Security number and the name of the person to be notified in case you are injured while working; these are questions that need not be asked until you're hired. You may feel that some of the questions have nothing to do with your ability to do the job you're seeking but are merely intrusions into your private business; is your ability to be judged on the expiration date on your driver's license or on whether you're married or not? And some of the questions may strike you as pointless: for what reason does the employer need to know your father's salary?

When filling out the application, you can also expect an assortment of questions about your health; you'll likely be asked if you've ever suffered such problems as dizzy spells, pains in the chest, worry or depression, sleepless nights, broken bones, and even thoughts of suicide.

Once you've completed the application, you'll be interviewed by the employer or a company official. Here, you can expect more personal questions—questions, for instance, about your ambitions, your likes and dislikes, and your political beliefs. In Robert Ellis Smith's book, *Privacy: How to Protect What's Left of It*, a California writer named Tom Nadeau tells of some of the personal probing he has endured in job interviews:

> "Interviewers have asked me to summarize my political views, to write my biography, to decribe myself in one sentence . . . to rate myself according to a chart on my aggressiveness, my determination to please and my loyalty."

Further, you may have to put up with some pretty personal advice from the interviewer. It is advice that can vary from interviewer to interviewer. Tom Nadeau continues:

> "I have been told . . . to cut my hair, let my hair grow, stand up straight, shave my mustache, grow a mustache, join a union, sign a paper saying I would not join a union . . . that I ought to dress better, that I ought to buy some more 'relaxed' clothes, that I was not creative enough, that I was too 'hip,' too square . . ."

Your most disquieting moments will likely come if you are among the countless job applicants who are asked each year to take a psychological or personality test. These tests, which are supposed to give the employer a better picture of you as a worker, are used by many companies, both large and small. They are famous for questions that are uncomfortably personal. A number inquire into the subject's sexual habits and characteristics. The tests have triggered widespread objections from applicants and labor unions.

In addition to asking one question after another, the employer may gather a wealth of information about you from outside sources—health records from doctors, a history of your debts and debt payments from credit bureaus, educational records from your schools, letters of recommendation from friends, clergymen, and former employers and teachers. By the time all is said and done, you may well feel that your life is an "open book" to someone or a company that may or may not decide to hire you.

You'll also understand that some of the questions are reasonable and that the employer has the right to ask them in an effort to gauge the kind of employee you'll make. And, regardless of your feelings about the most prying of the questions, you'll undoubtedly think that you *must* answer them, convinced that you'll harm your chances at winning a job if you refuse to do so. And you may be right. Your failure to coooperate may cause some employers to turn you down, as happened to the applicant who was not hired because he balked at answering the inquiries about his sex life in a California company's psychological test. In rejecting you, the company will probably not give you the actual reason for its decision but will come up with an excuse that won't trigger an argument on your part.

Now let's say that you survive all the probing. You land the job. On going to work, you're going to run into some more very common privacy problems.

YOUR SURROUNDINGS

When you arrive for your first day on the job, take a look at your surroundings. You may catch sight of some very modern electronic "snooping" gear in place up on the walls—small closed-circuit television cameras. They're principally found in businesses that serve the public—banks, department stores, specialty shops, restaurants, markets, and convenience stores.

Their official purpose is to keep an eye on the customers, detecting shoplifters and recording burglaries and robberies. The purpose is a sensible one because customer thievery, especially shoplifting, costs American businesses millions of dollars a year. But it is all too easy for employers to use the cameras to keep track of worker activities—to see who is lingering too long on coffee breaks, who is making personal telephone calls, who is treating customers rudely. Many labor unions, in negotiating contracts with employers, have insisted on including provisions that ban the use of the cameras for such "spying."

If you work in a department store, you may find that the mirrors in the fitting rooms are of the two-way variety. Again, the chief purpose is to detect customer thievery—to apprehend the customer who, as has happened in a number of instances, enters a fitting room with several items of wearing apparel, conceals them under his or her street clothing, and strolls out of the store; one New York department store stopped a woman as she was leaving while wearing six new dresses, one on top of the other. These same mirrors, however, can be used to spy on you should you enter a fitting room, perhaps on business, perhaps to have a few moments on your own. The stores that use the mirrors for such spying claim that they have a right to do so in the name of checking on worker efficiency. But, over the years, labor unions and many workers have argued that they should not be used for employee surveillance.

No matter where you work, you're going to find telephones close at hand. Many employers routinely listen in on and often record employee conversations. Their reasons for doing so are several: to check on the employee's telephone manners with customers, to determine that the phone system is working properly, to find if the employee is involved in some criminal activity with an outsider (such as plans to steal company merchandise), and to learn if any employee is using the telephone for extended private conversations. (Most companies do not object to necessary or emergency private calls, such as brief calls to see that a child has arrived safely home from school.)

As was explained in Chapter Four, the monitoring and/or recording of telephone calls with electronic devices—microphones, transmitters, and antennae—is called wiretapping. With certain exceptions, wiretapping and its companion activity, bugging, have been illegal since the 1960s unless carried out with a court order. Consequently, you may feel it your right to object if your employer monitors and/or records your telephone conversations. But your objection will go for naught. On two counts, private-sector employers are within their rights when they monitor and/or record employee phone calls. First, the federal Omnibus Crime Control and Safe Streets Act of 1968 and the laws in most states allow the recording of telephone conversations when one party or the other agrees to the recording, with the party who is making the recording not needing to inform the other of what is happening; your employer owns the telephone and, by listening to and recording your conversation, has agreed to the wiretap. (Not all states agree with this view, remember, with some, California among them, requiring the permission of both parties before a conversation can be recorded.) Second, employers are free to monitor personal calls by employees if the monitoring is done for what is called a valid business necessity.

Depending on your employer, you may find far more than your telephone calls being monitored. You may find that your desk is searched from time to time, perhaps in an effort to find evidence of some wrongdoing on your part; private-sector employers may legally look into desks without anybody's permission on the grounds that the desk is company property; workers in the public sector are granted some protections in this area. You may also find your boss poking his nose into your life away from work. Nosy bosses have long been a pain to employees in both the private and public sectors. There was a time when school boards would fire teachers who drank or smoked in their private lives. Henry Ford was famous not only for his automobiles but also for his curiosity about his workers' private lives; he had investigators look into such personal matters as the size of their families, their religious views, their ethnic backgrounds, their health, their hobbies, the amount of money they were saving, and even the neatness of their homes.

Modern versions of Henry Ford and old-time school districts are still to be found on the employment scene. There are employers who will not only forbid you to smoke in the workplace but will pressure you to stop smoking elsewhere as well; some will refuse to hire you or, as in the earlier-mentioned case of the Indiana woman, will even fire you. There are employers who will concern themselves with your mode of dress and hairstyle and will refuse to hire you or continue your employment if offended by either. There are employers who will keep close tabs on your life outside the workplace if you are heavily involved in the activities of your union. And employers who will want to know why you aren't contributing to the company's donations to a charitable cause, such as United Way.

These are all intrusions on your privacy—and some may strike you as discriminatory, such as the refusal to hire you because of your hairstyle. But there is little you can do about them, other than endure them, quit, or register a complaint with the employer or your union; such complaints may well end with the employer finding some reason to discharge you or, at the least, not promote you to a better job. The problem is that, while federal and state laws protect you from discriminatory actions by an employer, these intrusions are not considered to be discriminatory in any way.

But some intrusions *are* justified. If your job involves the safety of the public or your fellow employees, and you are found to have a drinking or a drug problem, the employer has the right and the duty to check it out and take steps to end it, perhaps by disciplining you, discharging you, or helping you by such means as counseling. The same, of course, holds true of any private problem that keeps you from doing your job properly.

Many employers are genuinely interested in the private lives of their employees but not for nosy reasons. You can count yourself fortunate if, in your lifetime, you work for employers who are interested in you as a person because they want to know that you're content in your work and want to help you solve any problems that may be troubling you. And you're especially lucky if you work for employers—and there are many of this type—who are sensitive to the privacy of both their applicants and employees. They ask the applicant mainly those questions that seek to learn the kind of worker he or she will be. They then take care not to concern themselves with those personal areas in an employee's life that have nothing to do with job performance.

A MATTER OF RECORD

Just as your school kept a record of your educational career, so will your employer keep a record of your work career. It will contain material ranging from your job application, letters of recommendation, and psychological test scores to performance evaluations by your superiors, complaints lodged against you, commendations for work well done, promotions, salary increases, and health and accident reports.

Many companies attempt to keep the material in employee records confidential, but it isn't always possible for them to do so. The requests for information are legion. When a worker applies for a job, the new company may request his or her records from earlier employers. Banks and/or credit bureaus request information when an employee takes out a loan. Researchers into economic and workplace problems want to study the records. Federal and state tax collectors request salary data. Federal and state agencies that oversee banking laws and regulate such activities as health care, welfare, transportation, commerce, and education—all need and request employee information for statistical purposes or for other aspects of their work.

As you know, the federal government's Family Educational Rights and Privacy Act enables you to check your school records. Matters are different for employment records. If you work for the federal government, you will be able to investigate your records under the provisions of the Privacy Act, which Congress enacted in 1974 and which is discussed in Chapter Eight. But, should you work for a private company or a state or local public agency, your ability to review your records will be determined by state law. Some states grant both their private and government employees the right of review. Others grant the right to all their government employees—from the local to the state level—but do not extend it to private workers. Still others grant the right only to the people who work for state agencies.

Many states have no laws at all pertaining to the review of work records. Here, if you wish to see your records, you will need to talk with your employer and seek his cooperation. It is a cooperation that may not be hard to obtain; many companies make it a policy to permit the reviews. You may also be allowed to see your records under the terms of the contract your union has arranged with your employer.

A SPECIAL PROBLEM

Let's say that you were once arrested or convicted for a crime. You may think that your chances of getting a job are pretty slim or even nonexistent.

Regardless of your feelings, go ahead and look for work. You will find that the Civil Rights Act of 1964 and the laws enacted by the states provide you with a number of helpful protections.

The safeguards vary according to whether you've been

arrested or convicted. An arrest means that the police had sufficient reason to suspect you of a crime and take you into custody; everything can end with the charges against you being dropped. A conviction means that you went to trial on the charges and were found guilty.

The nation's courts have long held that an employer who rejects applicants solely because they have arrest records is in violation of the Civil Rights Act (which applies only to companies with more than fifteen employees), particularly if he makes a habit of doing so. There are some jobs, though, in which the record is needed along with other data to provide the employer with enough information to judge the applicant's suitability; among them are jobs that involve the handling of drugs and large sums of money. However, an arrest record by itself is not seen by the courts and the laws in many states as sufficient grounds for denying employment.

You should check your state laws to see where you stand should the employer ask if you have an arrest record. Some states prohibit the asking of the question, either orally or in writing. Some states bar the question unless the employer can show that it must be asked because of the nature of the company's business (the handling of drugs, for instance).

What if you have a conviction in your past? Some states allow you to answer "no record" when an employer asks for word of any convictions. The reason for this is based on the idea that no one may be singled out for punishment outside the judicial system; therefore, the failure to be given a job for a conviction record is considered to be "punishment outside the judicial system." In at least one state— Massachusetts—you may reply "no record" if your convictions are for misdemeanors and are more than five years old.

Again, you should check your state laws to learn if questions about your arrest or conviction record can be asked and, if so, under what circumstances. And you'll be wise to check into your state laws to see what they have to say about having either record erased. You may find that you're entitled to ask the court to set the conviction aside—to declare that it never occurred—if it was for a first offense. Many states permit a conviction record to be destroyed after a given period of time, especially if the conviction was for a nonviolent offense. In common with some states, yours may permit a judge to seal your arrest record, an act that allows it then to be seen only by certain police officials—and only under certain circumstances.

How do you go about finding the needed state laws? You may write your representative in the state legislature for a copy of the laws. The local police may be able to advise or help you in your search. So may your local library. Or your family attorney.

Finally, you should check to find out what you can do to see your arrest or conviction record, review it for accuracy, and correct any errors you may unearth. It's wise to have an attorney's help here.

CHAPTER SEVEN

PRIVACY AND YOUR JOB:
Two Tests

At times in your working life, you may find yourself facing two tests, one or the other or both. Both are widely branded as invasions of the employee's privacy. They are the polygraph and urine tests.

POLYGRAPH TESTS

Polygraph tests, which take their name from the electronic mechanism used to administer them, are better known as lie detector tests. Should you ever take such a test, the examining technician will link you to the polygraph (by means of electrodes, rubber tubing, and a blood pressure cuff) and then ask a series of questions. Your answers will cause a set of pens to etch lines on a graph. Just as the lines drawn by a seismograph measure the intensity of an earthquake, the lines in the polygraph measure the intensity of three physiological changes that you experience when replying—changes in your blood pressure, breath rate, and perspiration. The intensity of the changes presumably indicate whether you are lying or telling the truth when answering certain of the questions.

The efforts to connect alterations in blood pressure, breath rate, and perspiration rate to the telling of falsehoods date back to the late nineteenth century. What was considered to be the first practical polygraph came into use in the 1920s. Ever since, the polygraph has been used by law enforcement agencies, medical personnel, and employers in both the public and private sectors. Its chief purpose in law enforcement has been to unmask or clear suspects in crimes. In the workplace—in large and small companies and businesses of every description—it has been used to detect untrustworthy applicants and employees suspected of theft or dishonesty. In both medicine and the workplace, it has measured the degree of stress in people needing or seeking psychiatric help. Employers usually have the test given by firms or individuals who specialize in its administration.

The American Civil Liberties Union (ACLU) reports that companies in the private sector annually asked upwards of 2 million employees and job applicants to take lie detector tests during the 1980s. The tests were meant to disclose matters ranging from employee theft to undesirable personality traits. The ACLU contends that the tests caused some 300,000 workers a year to be branded as liars and then fired, disciplined, or refused jobs.

The ACLU and privacy advocates across the nation have long criticized the polygraph test on several counts. To begin, they charge that it has been used by unscrupulous employers to harass certain workers. Enthusiastic union supporters and organizers have been among the targets here. So have "whistle blowers"—employees who have publicly reported faulty company products and unsafe practices.

Next, the critics of the test strongly oppose the indiscriminate use to which it has long been put in the workplace. Indiscriminate use means widespread testing that is conducted without justification and sometimes without prior warning. The critics argue that there must be a reasonable cause to suspect an employee of some misdeed before the polygraph can be brought into play.

Finally, they brand the polygraph test as an unreliable means of examination and an invasion of privacy.

The Question of Reliability

Among those who have long doubted the reliability of the polygraph test are the nation's courts. They agree with the general outlook that the accuracy of the test depends chiefly on the operator's expertise in interpreting what is indicated by the lines etched on the machine's graph. Since human error can play a major role in that interpretation, virtually all courts will not permit the results of polygraph testing to be used as evidence in trials.

Further, in the mid-1960s, a committee of the U.S. House of Representatives studied the polygraph and announced that there is no such thing as a lie detector, "neither machine nor human," adding that "people have been deceived by a myth that a metal box in the hands of an investigator can detect truth or falsehood." A decade later, the committee took another look at the polygraph and reached the same conclusion.

Privacy advocates agree with the committee's finding. They hold that the polygraph does not measure truthfulness but only changes in blood pressure and respiratory rate. These changes can be triggered by factors quite aside from the telling of a falsehood, factors that can include reactions of anger, fear, and embarrassment to the operator's questions. There is also the argument that a variety of medical conditions, such as colds and headaches, can lead to faulty results.

Polygraph operators claim that their machine is highly reliable and that it produces accurate results in 90 percent of its cases. Privacy advocates reply that 90 percent isn't good enough: 10 percent of the guilty can escape detection and 10 percent of the innocent can end up in trouble.

An Invasion of Privacy

The tests are accused of violating two of the constitutional amendments that pertain to privacy. They are said to violate the Fourth Amendment by "searching" the subject's mind with a wide range of questions, and the Fifth Amendment by asking questions that can lead the subject to incriminate himself or herself.

If you are just now entering work in the private sector, you are very fortunate so far as lie detector testing is concerned. In 1988, the U.S. Congress, in response to widespread complaints about the testing, enacted the Employee Polygraph Protection Act (EPPA). The Act protects most workers in the private sector from being forced to take the test.

It does so by prohibiting the use of polygraphs by private-sector companies that are involved in interstate commerce activities or in work affecting interstate commerce. Specifically, it states that these companies may not require, request, suggest, or, in any other way, cause an employee or a job applicant to submit to a polygraph test. Nor may they discharge, discipline, or discriminate against any employee or applicant who refuses to take the test.

The EPPA also outlaws the use of such variations on the polygraph machine as voice analyzers and the Psychological Stress Evaluator. They all attempt to detect the telling of lies by changes in the voice.

The Act, however, does permit private-sector employers to test employees under certain conditions. For one, a company may administer polygraph tests during an ongoing investigation into matters that may cause the company an economic loss or some other harm. Prime examples here would be investigations into the theft of company property or the leaking of company secrets to a competitor. But two prerequisites must be met before the tests can be given. First, the company must have sufficient grounds for suspecting that the employee to be tested is actually involved in the problem; perhaps, in the event of theft, he or she is one of the few who had access to the vanished goods. Second, the company must state in writing its reasons for suspecting the employee.

Under the Act, private firms that manufacture and distribute pharmaceuticals may test job applicants to ascertain, among other things, their possible abuse of drugs. Private security firms may also test applicants as part of a check for criminal activities in their backgrounds.

Left unprotected by the EPPA are government workers at the local, state, and federal levels. They have been excluded because studies show that they have not often been subjected to polygraph tests. It is estimated that, of the 2 million lie detector tests that were given annually to employees and job applicants during the 1980s, a mere 2 percent were ordered by government agencies. Further, government workers are less likely to be asked to take polygraph tests because they are protected by Civil Service regulations and by the laws in some states.

If you are ever asked to take a polygraph test, you should keep two points about the EPPA in mind. First, always remember that the Act prohibits the results of the test from being the sole basis on which your employer can take action against you. Should you, for instance, be tested for theft and appear to be guilty because you hesitate in answering a question, your employer may not use your "stumble" alone to fire or discipline you. He must join the results of the test with other evidence, all of it sound.

Next, when asked to take the test, remember that you are entitled to receive the following information beforehand from your employer:

- The date, hour, and location of the test.

- A list of the questions to be asked.

- The nature of the test to be given and the instruments to be used.

- A description of the testing area and word of whether a two-way mirror, camera, microphone, or other equipment will be used to observe you during the testing, plus notification that you or your employer may make a recording of the test if the consent of the other is obtained.

- The notification that you have the right to consult with an attorney or an employee representative before each phase of the test.

Then, when actually being questioned, you have the following rights:

- To stop the test at any time.
- Not be asked questions in a degrading or needlessly intrusive manner.
- Not to be asked about your religious, racial, and political beliefs and affiliations. Nor may you be questioned about your sexual activities. Nor about the lawful activities of your labor union.

Some employers have complained that, without the lie detector test, they will be less able to combat employee theft and dishonesty. The argument strikes critics of the polygraph as a weak one. They claim there is no solid evidence that the tests have ever actually reduced dishonesty and theft in the workplace. Prior to the passage of the EPPA, a number of states had laws restricting the use of polygraph testing. Research shows that they did not suffer a higher problem rate than the states in which the testing was permitted.

The test critics argue that there are better ways of preventing employee dishonesty and theft—ways that do not violate the privacy of the worker or the job applicant. Employers can protect themselves by such measures as checking references closely before hiring and by maintaining efficient security and inventory controls.

URINE TESTS

Millions of employees in both the public and private sectors are subjected to urine tests annually. The tests are designed to detect the presence of illegal drugs in a worker's system and often must be taken as a requirement for obtaining or keeping a job, especially a job having to do with the public safety (such as operating a train or flying an airliner) or with the manufacture or distribution of drug products. The tests yield either of two results—"positive," indicating that an illegal drug is present in the body, or "negative," indicating that it is absent. They have been widely used in the workplace ever since the abuse of drugs became a nationwide problem in the 1960s.

Indiscriminate urine testing—widespread testing that is carried out without justification—is strongly opposed by privacy advocates. Their reasons are the same as those that are applied to polygraph testing: it is unreliable and an invasion of privacy.

Why Unreliable?

Privacy advocates recognize that your employer has the right to expect that you not show up for work drunk, high, stoned, or too tired to do your job, and the right to know that your physical and mental condition will not endanger the public, your company's customers, or your fellow workers.

In our era of widespread drug abuse, the urine test might seem to be a wise strategy for combating the dangers that the abuse promises. But the privacy advocates contend that the test yields worthless results. The American Civil Liberties Union, in its informational publication, *ACLU Briefing Paper: Drug Testing in the Workplace*, presents the reasons for their argument:

> "Urine tests cannot determine *when* [author's italics] a drug was used. They can only detect the 'metabolites,' or inactive, leftover traces of previously ingested substances. For example, an employee who smokes marijuana on a Saturday night might test positive the following Wednesday, long after the drug has ceased to have any effect. In that case, what the employee did on Saturday has nothing to do with his or her fitness to work on Wednesday. At the same time, a worker can snort cocaine on the way to work and test negative the same morning. That is because the cocaine has not yet metabolized and will, therefore, not show up in the person's urine."

("Metabolize" means that an ingested substance has built up sufficiently in the bloodstream to pass into the urine.)

> ". . . the drug screens used by most companies are not reliable. These tests yield false positive results at least 10 percent, and possibly as much as 30 percent of the time. Experts concede that the tests are unreliable. At a recent conference, 120 forensic scientists, including some who worked for manufacturers of drug tests, were asked, 'Is there anybody who would submit urine for drug testing if his career, reputation, freedom or livelihood depended on it?' Not a single hand was raised."

The ACLU publication goes on to remark that more accurate tests are available on the market but that they are not widely used because they are expensive. But even these tests, despite their accuracy, can yield inaccurate results, this due to errors made by the laboratory workers who screen the urine specimens.

"A survey by the National Institute of Drug Abuse, a government agency, found that 20 percent of the labs surveyed mistakenly reported the presence of illegal drugs in drug-free urine samples. Unreliability also stems from the tendency of drug screens to confuse similar chemical compounds. For example, codeine and Vicks Formula 44-M have been known to produce positive results for heroin, Advil for marijuana, and Nyquil for amphetamines."

Why an Invasion of Privacy?

Indiscriminate use of the urine test, in common with the indiscriminate use of the polygraph test, is said to violate the Fourth and Fifth amendments—and for the very same reasons: it constitutes an unreasonable search and puts the subjects in danger of incriminating themselves.

Further, the urine test is usually taken it the presence of a witness. The purpose of the witness is to prevent the subject from tampering with the sample and getting a favorable result. This necessitates that the subject suffer the embarrassment of performing a highly private function in front of another party.

(Some people wonder how test subjects may tamper with urine samples. A commonplace method of tampering has long been known in athletics. When professional or amateur athletes are informed that they are to be tested for steroids or some other substance, many will obtain a urine sample from a friend, conceal it in their clothing, and then surreptitiously substitute it for their own during the test.)

Opponents of the test experienced a setback in 1989. That year, in cases involving railroad workers and customs guards, the U.S. Supreme Court ruled that these government workers could legally be made to take urine tests even though not suspected of drug use. The Court admitted that the test is a search but that public safety and the government's intention to maintain a workplace free of drugs far outweighs the workers' rights under the Fourth Amendment.

Despite the Court's decision, workers in the public sector have some protections against the test. Many state and federal courts have declared that indiscriminate urine testing of government workers is unconstitutional on the basis that it violates the Fourth Amendment by being an unreasonable search of the body; there must be adequate grounds for suspicion before the government employee can be subjected to the test. There are state laws against indiscriminate testing in the private sector, but unfortunately they are few and far between. Several states—among them Montana, Iowa, and Vermont—have banned the practice altogether. A handful of others, such as Minnesota and Maine, allow random testing (meaning the testing of randomly picked employees) only for their private and public employees whose jobs affect public or company safety; included among such employees are airline pilots and workers in nuclear plants.

As a private employee, you are most fortunate if you live in California. The state's constitution contains a right-to-privacy provision that severely restricts the testing and other intrusions into the lives of both private and public employees.

Other than California's constitutional provision and the few laws that have been mentioned above, you are virtually without any protections against urine tests in the private workplace. You can only hope that your labor union, in its contract with your employer, has managed to prohibit or place heavy restrictions on their use.

CHAPTER EIGHT

PRIVACY AND THE COMPUTER

There was a time when any personal information that was gathered about us—from our name and address on a job application to the grades we earned in school—was typed on a piece of paper and tucked away in a file cabinet, there to join other pieces of paper about us. It could remain there for years and, often forgotten, never reach the outside world.

Things have done a complete about-face since then. Responsible for the change has been the astonishingly swift development in recent years of that "super electronic device of the century"—the computer. Today, any data that is collected about us in one place or another—and for one reason or another—can be stored in a computer bank. It can then be easily passed to other computer banks—banks of all sizes that are now to be found throughout the nation. They are owned by individuals and by private businesses and corporations, lending institutions, direct mailing and telemarketing firms, credit bureaus, credit card companies, charitable and religious organizations, school systems and universities, and government agencies at the local, state, and federal level.

The amount of personal information that goes into computer banks can stagger the imagination. Some idea of that amount can be had by looking at a list of the data that may one day be kept on file about you in the computers of one type of company:

- Name, address, telephone number, age
- Social Security number
- Name of current employer, your salary, and length of employment
- Former employer
- Automobile loan and history of payments
- Home mortgage and history of payments
- Credit status in local stores
- Bank loans and history of payments
- Credit cards and history of payments
- Court actions against you for nonpayment of loans and credit purchases within the past five years
- Repossessions of merchandise that you purchased on credit and then failed to pay
- Credit accounts so far in arrears that the lender hired a collection agency to secure the money due

Records such as these are maintained by credit bureaus, which, as you'll recall, maintain files on your financial history. Whenever you buy something on credit—from a purchase in a store to the purchase of a home—the records are used by the seller to determine whether you are a good risk to pay the money owed. The records are also made available to insurance companies to see if you can pay for the coverage you seek, and to prospective employers who hope the information will give them some insight into your reliability as a worker.

Credit bureaus are found in cities and towns everywhere and are recognized as among the largest collectors of data in the nation. Many are local firms. Just as many are branches of nationally owned companies.

The list of hands into which computerized personal information can now fall seems as endless as the range of data that can be housed in the computer banks. In all, the "super electronic device of the century" is charged with making our lives an open book to millions of people—from those who feed and operate the banks to those who obtain the stored data for business, governmental, personal, or other reasons.

A growing number of Americans are seeing the accumulation and distribution of computerized data as a frightening invasion of their privacy. Surveys show that the number of worried Americans has been steadily growing through recent years as the computer becomes increasingly efficient, easier to operate, and less costly to purchase and maintain. In 1970, a national survey showed that 37 percent of the people questioned felt their privacy was being invaded. Seven years later, 47 percent expressed the same worry. A 1990 survey, which was conducted by one of the country's largest credit bureaus, revealed that the number of alarmed citizens had shot up to 76 percent.

Aside from the massive amount of material that is involved, the use of the computer for the storage of personal data is widely condemned on a number of counts. First, the information can then easily get into the hands of individuals and organizations that have neither a right nor a reason to see it. Author Jeffrey Rothfeder, in his book *Privacy for Sale: How Computerization Has Made Everyone's Private Life an Open Secret*, writes of one well-known case of personal information being obtained by someone who had no business seeing it.

In 1987, federal judge Robert Bork was being considered for a position on the U.S. Supreme Court. A Washington, D.C., newspaper reporter went to the video store where Bork was a regular customer and asked for a list of the films that the judge had rented. The clerk pulled the list from the store's computer and handed it to the reporter, who had obviously hoped that it would contain the names of some X-rated films. On the list, however, were mainly John Wayne films.

Innocent though the list proved to be, the reporter's paper went ahead and published it. Members of Congress were angered by this pointless invasion of privacy and, in 1988, enacted the Video Privacy Protection Act. The Act prohibits video rental stores from disclosing a customer's rentals without either the customer's consent or a court order. Also, the stores cannot build and sell lists that are based on customer rental records.

The criticisms include the charge that it is all too easy to store out-of-date personal information in the computer—information that can be damaging to the subject. A case in point:

In 1977, a young salesman was turned down for the post of sales manager with a midwestern company because of an entry that had been made in his employment record five years earlier while he was working for a department store. The entry went into his record after he had been photographed taking part in a demonstration against the Vietnam War and branded him a "radical," a term that, in the minds of many, automatically means a "troublemaker."

Today, the man says, "I opposed the U.S. involvement in Vietnam, just as many other perfectly loyal Americans did. I was in college at the time and a lot of students were demonstrating against the war. By the time I applied for the sales manager job, I was long gone from college. I was married and had a family. I had become conservative in my political views. The term "radical" just didn't apply to me anymore—if it ever did in the first place. But it still lost me a job."

Another major criticism holds that mistaken data is allowed to get into the computer banks. In *Privacy: How to Protect What's Left of It*, Robert Ellis Smith points out that the errors are many, even legion, and can range from the silly to the extremely serious. On the silly side of things, he reports what an Ohio man saw some years after asking to see the report that a credit bureau had prepared on him:

"When Richard Brudzynski of Cleveland checked his file he was surprised to learn that the credit report listed him as a stock clerk, previously employed as an attorney. In fact, Brudznynski worked as a stock clerk before he became a lawyer. A bachelor, he was even more surprised to learn that the credit file listed him as married—to, of all people, his own mother."

Though the report was silly, the same certainly cannot be said of other examples. Consider what happened some years ago to a retired speech writer in Virginia. As reported in a November issue of *Time* magazine, he was bewildered when a local bank rejected his request for a loan. He then learned that a subsidiary of a national credit bureau had been merging his credit history with that of a man with the same name—but a man who had a string of bad debts. The writer spent weeks working on the mix-up with the credit bureau and thought that he had finally cleared up the matter—only to be turned down for a loan in 1990, at which time he found that his file had again been invaded with information about the man with the same name.

Quite as serious—and perhaps even more so—are the following examples from Robert Ellis Smith's *Privacy: How to Protect What's Left of It*. The first concerns what happened to several innocent people when mistakes occurred in a giant computer bank of criminal information that is operated by the Federal Bureau of Investigation. It is known as the National Crime Information Center (NCIC):

" . . . a California couple spent the night in jail because the computer system reported that they were driving a stolen car. They were. The car had been stolen a year earlier and returned to the rightful owners . . ."

"A young man riding in an auto in Dallas was arrested and held for four hours because an NCIC report showed him absent without leave from the Marines. In fact, he had been discharged from the military three months earlier after AWOL [Absent Without Official Leave] charges were dropped. The confusion was resolved and he was released."

The young man may have been released, but what happened to him a short time later points up another major danger that lurks in the maintenance of computerized data—the frequent failure to remove mistaken data after it has been shown to be in error:

"Within six months, he was stopped while hitchhiking and detained for twenty-four hours because the NCIC still recorded him as AWOL. Four months after that, he was driving . . . and locked up for four hours because the FBI's computer system still showed him AWOL."

One of the most tragic examples given by Smith does not concern the NCIC bank but an erroneous entry that made its way into a state computer system:

" . . . When a young couple in Milwaukee took their newborn infant to a hospital with eleven fractured bones, they were accused of child abuse. The parents were duly reported to a county child abuse information system and eventually to a statewide system. [You'll recall from an earlier chapter that the law requires all cases of child abuse, suspected or actual, be reported to the authorities.] The county welfare department sought to remove the child from the parents' custody. The two insisted on their innocence . . . A doctor suggested they get psychiatric help. A social worker predicted they would be divorced before long."

The charge that the young husband and wife were guilty of child abuse was eventually proved to be in error, Smith writes, "when a specialist finally determined that the baby was actually suffering from a rare metabolic birth defect—terminal in nature—that makes the bones extremely weak and brittle. There had been no beatings." But, because of the error, the young couple had endured for months a nightmare that humiliated them and threatened them with the heartbreaking loss of their child.

The people who operate and maintain computer banks like to insist that the material in their banks is safe from invasion by outsiders. But the truth of the matter is that the banks, as in the Robert Bork case, can be invaded and their data removed. Many of the invasions have been for criminal purposes. Jeffrey Rothfeder, in *Privacy for Sale*, proves the point with a startling example:

He writes of gangs that come to the United States from Nigeria. On arriving here, they seek jobs as security guards. The jobs are low-paying and are easy to land because employers find them hard to fill. On being assigned to commercial buildings at night, the members rummage through file cabinets, desks, and the office computers to pick up personal employee data that ranges from names, addresses, and Social Security numbers to job titles and earnings. Rothfeder explains that, according to the fraud division of the United States Secret Service, they use the data to obtain credit cards with phony applications. With the cards, they purchase merchandise worth thousands of dollars and rent expensive cars. Then, before the innocent victims or the authorities know what has happened, the gangs ship everything back to Nigeria, there to be sold for a hefty profit.

Rothfeder adds that, according to a memo by one of the country's leading credit bureaus, the gangs pull off as many as 100,000 such deals each year.

GOVERNMENT ACTIONS

The criticisms leveled against the computer caused the U.S. Congress to take several actions in the 1970s. Two of the most important dealt with the computerization of personal information collected by credit bureaus and the federal government. It is vital that you know about each in the event that you ever need to take steps to protect yourself on suspecting or finding that personal and potentially damaging information about you is housed in some credit bureau or federal file.

The Fair Credit Reporting Act

In 1970, the U.S. Congress enacted a measure intended to correct the misuse and abuse of personal data collected by credit bureaus (and any company that provides them with data)—The Fair Credit Reporting Act (FCRA). The Act requires the bureau to follow three basic rules:

- It may not report "obsolete information" about you. Obsolete information is defined as data that is more than seven years old. There is an exception here. If you ever declare bankruptcy, the time limit for reporting it is set at fourteen years.

- The bureau may not lift information on you from an earlier report and use it without checking into it and establishing its accuracy.

■ On your request, the bureau must disclose "the nature and substance of all information" on you contained in its files.

If you wish to check on the information in a credit report, you should locate the credit bureau in your area. You may then go to the bureau or have the information given to you over the telephone. If you choose the latter course, you must first write to the bureau and verify your identity.

Suppose that, on looking at your report, you find some data with which you disagree—perhaps a mistaken entry claiming you still owe a department store bill that was paid months ago. The bureau must investigate the entry immediately and, if indeed there is a mistake, remove it from the record. But, if there is a dispute over the entry—say, the department store insists that the bill is still unpaid and you cannot present proof to the contrary—you are allowed to attach to the report a brief statement explaining your side of the dispute. The statement may be no more than 100 words in length.

Further, the FCRA permits you to look into the reasons why you were refused credit, an insurance policy, or a job as the result of a credit report. Whoever refused you is required to give you the name of the bureau that prepared the damaging report.

The Act has been of help to many people as they seek to make purchases on credit, take out insurance policies, or apply for work. But privacy advocates find it a weak measure on several counts. For one, they contend that it does not require a credit bureau, despite the mandate for "a complete and accurate disclosure," to turn over all the information in your file. Rather, the bureau, though it may provide every scrap of that information if it so chooses, is required to supply you only with a summary of the data.

Further, the FCRA contains no provision for penalizing the bureau that discloses obsolete or incorrect data. All that is required is that the bureau be able to show that it has established "reasonable procedures" to prevent mistaken or obsolete information from getting into its reports.

Privacy advocates especially dislike the fact that the FCRA covers only credit bureaus and the companies that provide them with information. Other persons or organizations go ignored, meaning that anyone who is not connected with a credit bureau can obtain or develop records of your past history of bill paying without being bound by the requirements of the Act.

The Privacy Act

As was pointed out in Chapter One, the federal government is the greatest collector of personal records. A count taken in 1982 (the last time such a count was made) showed that the federal government held 3.5 billion records on American citizens—for an average of 15 files for every man, woman, and child in the country. The total is certain to have risen in the years since. In *Privacy for Sale*, Jeffrey Rothfeder reports that 178 of the largest federal offices (meaning both federal departments and agencies) operate some 2,000 computer banks, with each containing tens of millions of files.

In 1974, the U.S. Congress enacted a law that enables citizens to check their federal records to see if they are correct and to take steps to have any erroneous entries corrected—the Privacy Act. The Act permits the checks to be made only by individuals and not by businesses and corporations. It defines an individual as a United States citizen or a lawful permanent resident alien.

Heading the list of the Act's provisions are the following three:

- You are allowed to look at your federal records on request.

- The information placed in your federal records must be "accurate and timely."

- Federal offices must make lists of the people who request to see your records and must make those lists available to you on request.

Several points must always be remembered about the Act. It opens the way for you to investigate only your federal records. Not within your reach under the terms of the measure are any files held by state or local governments or by private organizations. There is, however, a major exception here. Within reach are the records being accumulated for a federal office by a private organization.

There are also a number of federal offices that are not required to turn over your records for perusal. In the main, these offices work in law enforcement or in matters involving the national security. One is the Central Intelligence Agency. Another is the Secret Service; no demand can be made on it to release any files pertaining to the protection of the president. Also, the Federal Bureau of Investigation need not turn over certain of its files.

Many of the federal files are used to review government

programs and to determine who is eligible for benefits under those programs. You may want to examine any that pertain to you if you ever, for instance, apply for a student loan, a veteran's loan, or a Social Security benefit. Also on file are records that cover such diverse individuals as drug patients, blood donors, and farmers. One office keeps records of federal employees who suffer traffic accidents in government cars. The names and addresses of offices with data banks are contained in the *United States Government Manual* and in the annual lists published by the *Federal Register*. These sources are to be found in most public libraries.

Should you suspect or learn that your name is in a federal office computer, you should first ask the office if indeed such a file does exist. The office is required to provide the answer.

If you receive an affirmative reply, you can immediately request that the file be made available for your inspection. You may make your request by letter or telephone call, or by appearing in person at the office. (If you make an office call, you may go by yourself or in the company of a friend or adviser.) The American Civil Liberties Union advises that you write a letter and keep a copy of it in your possession, along with all correspondence received in return. In this way, you will have a complete record of your request in the event there is some mix-up or difficulty later on.

When writing the letter, you should give your full name and permanent address, plus any other names you may have used in the past. You do not need to give further information at this time, though the office may later ask for additional information to help in the search for the file. Above all, you need not give the reason for your request.

Simply state that you want to see your file. You are not required by law to justify your request; it is your right to see the file.

You must, however, be prepared to verify your identity. The office must take steps to ascertain that it never violates someone's privacy by mistakenly handing that person's file over to you. You are open to criminal penalties if you knowingly obtain or try to obtain another's record.

The office must give you a copy of the record in a form that you can understand; this means that all computer codes and shorthand symbols in it must be transformed into understandable English. Then, should you find an error on reading the file, you are entitled to take the same steps that are open to you under the Fair Credit Reporting Act and the Family Educational Rights and Privacy Act (see Chapter Five). First, you can demand that the error be corrected, after which it will be reviewed by a government official. Next, if the error remains in dispute and uncorrected at the end of the review, you can write a statement explaining your side of things. The statement, as is also stipulated in the other two Acts, is to be made a permanent part of the record.

There are two additional federal measures that you should know about in connection with federal records. The first is the Freedom of Information Act (FOIA), which was passed into law by Congress in 1966. It requires that federal offices make a wide range of their records available to the public. The FOIA differs from the Privacy Act in that it opens the records to the public, while the latter enables individuals to inspect their own files.

The second is the Tax Reform Act of 1976. This measure

bars the Internal Revenue Service from looking into your bank records without your knowledge. Before conducting such a search, the Service must notify you of what is planned and secure a court order for the investigation. Remember, however, that the Act applies only to federal tax officials. It does not prevent the FBI, private businesses, and federal, state, and local law enforcement officers from looking into your bank records.

State Measures

Many states—Arkansas, California, Connecticut, and Massachusetts among them—have enacted laws in keeping with the Privacy Act. The laws permit you to examine your records that are held by state government offices and, if necessary, call for them to be corrected. If you wish to check these records, you should first determine whether the laws in your state will permit you to do so. The laws usually exclude the examination of law enforcement records.

CHAPTER NINE

PROTECTING EVERYONE'S PRIVACY:
What You Can Do

This book has concentrated on what we can do to protect ourselves as individuals in a time when the invasion of privacy is a widespread and continually growing problem. The protection of our individual selves, however, can do no more than solve a part of the problem. We need also to work for the protection of all the people around us—from our loved ones to the millions of fellow citizens we will never meet in our lifetimes. Only by protecting everyone else can we possibly hope to end today's growing threat to our privacy. It is a threat that, if left unchecked, could well turn us into the society that novelist George Orwell envisioned in *1984*.

But what can we do to protect the right to privacy now and in the years to come? We can do much by taking a few simple steps.

1. LEARN ALL YOU CAN ABOUT THE PROBLEM

By reading this book, you've taken your first step here.

But the reading of a single book does not mean that you've learned *everything* about the current threats to our privacy. By itself, no book can tell you all there is to know about a topic. Further, there are bound to be occurrences, political developments, and technological advances that will intensify the problem in the future. Constant study is necessary to keep abreast of all that is happening today and that may happen in the future.

To find the books, magazine articles, and newspaper reports that can help you learn more of the problem, consult the bibliography that follows this chapter. Its every entry can provide you with much valuable information. Then, to stay alert to current and future developments, read your daily newspaper and check your local library from time to time to find the latest books and magazine articles on the subject. The reference librarian will be happy to help you in your search.

2. SHARE WHAT YOU LEARN WITH OTHERS

There are many things you can do to share your knowledge of the problem with others. To begin, you can talk with the members of your family; the topic can be a fascinating one for dinner table conversation. Next, of course, there are all sorts of possibilities for sharing at school. You can bring up the right to privacy for classroom discussion; the same can be done in your social studies or civics club. There is nothing to stop you from gathering several friends together and presenting a classroom or assembly program on how that right is being threatened today. You can write an article for your school newspaper. One of the most important steps that can be taken is to interest your classmates and neighborhood friends in what is going on so that they will want to spread the word to their families and friends.

3. TAKE POLITICAL ACTION

On learning that Congress, your state legislature, or a local governing body is considering the enactment of a measure pertaining to privacy, write to your representatives. Let them know that you support or oppose the measure—and why. Urge them to vote for or against it. It's their job to listen to what the public says. Most people speak out eloquently and vehemently on measures that they oppose. Add your voice to theirs against any measure that threatens the preservation of personal privacy, but be sure to speak out just as strongly for measures that seek to safeguard it.

4. MAINTAIN YOUR INTEREST

We've all had the experience of having various interests —hobbies, say, and activities—fall by the wayside as others have come along to catch our eye. It would be sad if this happened to your current interest in safeguarding our privacy. It is too important a subject to be forgotten or replaced by other interests. And so, make every effort to carry your present enthusiasm into your adulthood. Our country's passion for collecting personal information for commercial, political, and various other reasons—plus the developing technologies that will make the collecting all the easier in the future—will surely trouble us for years to come. The job of guarding our right to privacy and speaking out against the assault on it is going to be a lifelong one.

5. EXERCISE SYMPATHY AND CONSIDERATION

While concentrating on protecting the right to privacy, take pains to see that you never make a mistake that can be all too easily made and that *is* made, sometimes daily, by countless people. Do not thoughtlessly or deliberately violate the privacy of another person. This final suggestion returns us to a point that was made in Chapter Four, when we were speaking of privacy in the family. Family members who respect your privacy all share two characteristics in common—a sympathy for and a consideration of your feelings. The two can serve as the keystone for solving all the privacy problems that may crop up in anyone's everyday life—at home, at school, at work, among friends and relatives, and out in the community. You can use these two characteristics to greet with kindness everyone's need and desire for privacy while setting an example that, without saying a word, will lead others to greet your same need and desire with the same kindness.

BIBLIOGRAPHY

Books

Atkinson, Linda. *Your Legal Rights*. New York: Franklin Watts, 1982.

Brill, Alida. *Nobody's Business: Paradoxes of Privacy*. Reading, Massachusetts: Addison-Wesley, 1990.

Dolan, Edward F. *Legal Action: A Layman's Guide*. Chicago: Regnery, 1972.

————. *Protect Your Legal Rights: A Handbook for Teenagers*. New York: Julian Messner, 1983.

Goode, Stephen. *The Right to Privacy*. New York: Franklin Watts, 1983.

LeMond, Alan and Fry, Ron. *No Place to Hide*. New York: St. Martin's Press, 1975.

Lieberman, Jethro K. *Privacy and the Law*. New York: Lothrop, Lee & Shepard, 1978.

McClellan, Grant M. *The Right to Privacy*. New York: H. H. Wilson, 1976.

Meltzer, Milton. *The Bill of Rights: How We Got It and What It Means*. New York: Thomas Y. Crowell, 1990.

Petrocelli, William. *Low Profile: How to Avoid the Privacy Invaders*. New York: McGraw-Hill, 1981.

Rothfeder, Jeffrey. *Privacy for Sale: How Computerization Has Made Everyone's Private Life an Open Secret.* New York: Simon & Schuster, 1992.

Shattuck, John H. F. *Rights of Privacy.* Skokie, Illinois: National Textbook Company in conjunction with the American Civil Liberties Union, 1977.

Smith, Robert Ellis. *Privacy: How to Protect What's Left of It.* New York: Anchor Books/Doubleday, 1980.

Strouse, Jean. *Up Against the Law: The Legal Rights of People Under Twenty-One.* New York: New American Library, 1970.

Westin, Alan. *Privacy and Freedom.* New York: Atheneum, 1967.

Wicklein, John. *Electronic Nightmare: The New Communications and Freedom.* New York: Viking, 1981.

Magazines

Beck, Melinda. "Video Vigilantes," *Newsweek*, July 22, 1991.

"How Do I Stop Junk Mail?" *Modern Maturity*, December 1992–January 1993.

Lacayo, Richard. "Nowhere to Hide," *Time*, November 11, 1991.

Larson, Erik. "Espionage in the Marketplace," *Smithsonian*, January 1993.

Linowe, David F. "Privacy in America Update: The Individual's Right to Legal Action," *Vital Speeches of the Day*, January 15, 1991.

"The Privacy Invaders: Who Knows What About You?" *Good Housekeeping*, November 1989.

Sanders, Alain L. "Reach Out and Tape Someone," *Time*, January 8, 1990.

Seligman, Daniel. "The Devil in Direct Marketing," *Fortune*, March 11, 1991.

Zoglin, Richard. "Justice Faces a Screen Test," *Time*, June 17, 1991.

Newspapers

Arnold, Jay. "Phone Device Causes Worry about Privacy," *San Francisco Chronicle* (from Associated Press), January 2, 1990.

Calandra, Tom. " 'Privacy for Sale': Tales of Data Rape," *San Francisco Examiner*, September 13, 1992.

Carnevale, Mary Lu and Lopez, Julie Amparano. "Making a Phone Call Might Mean Telling the World about You," *Wall Street Journal*, November 28, 1989.

Foltz, Kim. "Firms Snooping on Shoppers," *San Francisco Chronicle* (from *New York Times*), December 18, 1989.

Booklets, Pamphlets, Papers

The Privacy Act: How It Affects You and How to Use It. New York: American Civil Liberties Union, undated.

Surveillance: Is This the Law? New York: American Civil Liberties Union, undated.

Understanding Civil Liberties: A Guide for the Perplexed. New York: New York Civil Liberties Union, Nassau Chapter, 1989.

ACLU Briefing Paper: The Rights of Employees. New York: American Civil Liberties Union, undated.

ACLU Briefing Paper: Lie Detector Testing. New York: American Civil Liberties Union, undated.

ACLU Briefing Paper: Drug Testing in the Workplace. New York: American Civil Liberties Union, undated.

ACLU Briefing Paper: The Right to Choose—A Fundamental Freedom. New York: American Civil Liberties Union, undated.

ACLU Briefing Paper: A History of the Bill of Rights. New York: American Civil Liberties Union, undated.

INDEX

Index

Index